**KU-472-791**

This book is a gift to you from Scottish Book Trust, a national charity changing lives through reading and writing, to celebrate Book Week Scotland (16–22 November 2020).

**bookweekscotland.com**

*Future* is a collection of true stories written by the people of Scotland. This book is one of 50,000 **free** copies – thank you for picking it up! If you enjoy it, help us share it with as many people as possible. Dip into it and share a few favourites with friends, display it, gift a copy to a partner, colleague or parent, or even leave it somewhere for a stranger to discover. (We recommend a reading age of 15+.)

These stories are both funny and moving, paying tribute to the breadth of storytelling across multiple generations all over Scotland. We hope you enjoy them.

Happy reading!

#BookWeekScotland

A huge thank you to the following supporters,
including all those who wish to remain anonymous.

## Supported the production and gifting of this book

Alice Ruby Foulis

Laura Talbot

## Left a gift in their will to Scottish Book Trust

Estate of A R Taylor

## Supported Scottish Book Trust as members of
## The Book Club

Christian Albuisson

Lucy Juckes and Ben Thomson

Marian and Mark Deere

Martin Adam and William Zachs

Scott Lothian

# Future

scottishbooktrust.com

First published in 2020 by Scottish Book Trust, Sandeman House, Trunk's Close, 55 High Street, Edinburgh EH1 1SR

scottishbooktrust.com

The authors' right to be identified as an author of this book under the Copyright, Patents and Designs Act 1988 has been asserted

A CIP catalogue record for this book is available from the British Library

Typeset by Laura Jones

Printed and bound by CPI Group (UK) Ltd, Croydon CR0 4YY

Scottish Book Trust makes every effort to ensure that the paper used in this book has been legally sourced from well-managed and sustainable forests

Cover design by O Street

This is a free book, designed to be read alone or in groups, enjoyed, shared and passed on to friends. This book is gifted to you by Scottish Book Trust for Book Week Scotland 2020

Digital editions of this book are available from scottishbooktrust.com/future

# Contents

## Lockdown reflections

## Hopes for a new decade

*Stories by published authors.*
*Please be aware that this book is unsuitable for readers aged 14 or younger as it contains strong language and mature content.*

# This is Now
## by Val McDermid

We are living in a time of chaos. We are living in a time of fear. We are living in a time of uncertainty.

What we need now is the confidence to rewrite the script. But if we're truly going to do that, we need imagination. We need to imagine both what will happen if we sit back and do nothing and also what could happen if we challenge the future and change it.

But change doesn't happen by chance. It happens because first we have the courage to be creative in picturing the world we want to live in, and then living as if we believe that world is possible.

It's not always easy to express these ideas or work out how they can be put into effect. That's where the power of imagination steps in. Whether it's poets, novelists, lyricists, short story writers, essayists or writers of narrative non-fiction and journalism, writers bring us a lucky bag of possibilities.

We don't have to agree with them; indeed, it's often these moments of disagreement that crystallise our ideas more than anything else. Provocation is the best call to action; at least, it always has been for me.

Now more than ever we need to give space to the voices of young people and to listen to what they have to say. The inheritance we've bequeathed is not one of promise;

it's problematic as far as the mind's eye can see. But the gift of youth is possibility, of ideas and ideals, of hope. And of determination.

Asking young writers to harness their imagination and create work that focuses on the future is an opportunity to take the first steps in a different direction. When this time capsule is opened in ten years, it will serve as a benchmark for us, to see whether we have accepted the challenges of today or run away from them. Either way, it will be worth waiting for!

*See You in Ten Years*

Further writing from Val McDermid will appear in our Book Week Scotland time capsule homed at the National Library of Scotland and due to be opened in 2030. The time capsule has been made by Ali Forbes and contains a copy of this book, plus further stories on the theme of future written by young people across Scotland.

# Celebrating now

# Hefting to the Land
**Annie Sturgeon**

I live in the Howe, a hollow surrounded by hills, where
calling geese can circle all night in a bowl of winter
fog that has the density of porridge, but where now,
intense yellow broom lights a glowing edge the colour
of free-range egg yolks around the rim. The river Don
runs through it, west to east. Not a huge river but quite
fast flowing and you can't cross it on foot. It's clear
and bright, the colour of polished pewter. My side is
north of the river. My home is surrounded by fields of
sheep brought inbye for the lambing, below a ridge of
mixed woodland where buzzards nest. The pot-holed
roads are barely more than single-track, quiet with only
farm vehicles and the postie van now. I know that I am
fortunate. I know this.

Our old granite house has a one-acre garden protected
by huge trees and granite walls. It's full of plants;
domesticated and wild. We have two dogs and six hens;
free to roam their world. There are established fruit trees
and bushes, and newly planted vegetables growing in
rich, well-tended soil. The air is fresh, clean and light;
lichens testify to that. Sometimes, there are smells of
beasts or earthy rain, daphne or honeysuckle, rosemary,
tarragon or golden marjoram and clover flowers of
honey scent to succour the senses. And gorse, with its
scent of coconut and almonds, fills the air on warm,
calm days. And birds: the air is full of birds and their
songs and calls now. I hear them above other world
music. I roll along with it, beside it and within it. I know
that I am fortunate. I know this.

My community is growing with the shrinking;
restricted in terms of travel, distances no more now.
We are becoming aware. We are smiling; greeting over
garden gates, speaking as we cross the road, connecting
in WhatsApp groups, caring that we all have everything
we need and more (like the nest boxes Theo is making
for us all despite his blindness), sharing the joy and
sorrow of a granddaughter not yet held. We are owning
each other, reaching out and reaching in. We're creating
a web, of security and contentment. Learning to value
each other and where we are. We're discovering who we
are, who is around us. Not what they are or who they
strove to be. We are shedding outer layers, removing
personal shields (whilst shielding), letting them slowly
fall away; we are revealing and letting in a light. We
touch, without touching. We are embracing; 2 metres
apart. I know that I am fortunate. I know this.

I sense that I am moving in a time that's a reflection
of 150 years ago; at the pace of the Shire horse, the
pace of a laden donkey. I'm trundling along on my
Tramper. Listening to breezes through the crab apple
blossom flanking the old drove road, watching pink
petals floating like confetti on my union with this life
now. This warm breeze has time to ruffle hair and bring
butterflies for me to notice. I have time to watch buds
unfurl and insects pollinating. I have time to listen
to all the different calls of each bird and their young.
I have time to smell the scents of the gorse and the
woolly, blooded scent of newborn lambs that we drove
past with the windows closed this time last year; and
to notice their roughly wrinkled skin. I am aware now
of the smaller things like speedwell; bright blue bird's-
eyes peering through the sweet green of fresh grass. All
these things were there before, always present, rarely

observed, essential to our lives; to my life. I know that I am fortunate. I know this.

And when the lockdown's over I'll be hefted to this land, like the sheep.

**Author story note:** *I was out on my mobility scooter taking my assistance dog for a walk, riding along the country lanes and round the fields, just me and her. It was a beautiful day. I was travelling at walking pace for about an hour, and really starting to notice things around me. When I stopped by the crab apple trees along the old drove road, and their blossom started falling, I felt a new connection and recognised that this lockdown situation had begun to provide a positive future for me and others, a new normal, that I wanted to maintain.*

# Cherish
**Ruth Gilchrist**

Yesterday a storm blew,
Today I learn poems.
Tomorrow I cherish.

Tomorrow we will go again to visit cherry trees.
Cup blossom in gloved hands
count the petals.

We will wear fine clothes and remove our shoes at the
   door.
Bring gifts of air and sunbeams,
prune out the news.

We will water them from a galvanised bucket,
feed them with unrushed listening.
Share leaves with our friends.

We will make studies in the ways of their roots,
idols of their dedicated pollinators,
be mindful of their wounds.

We will choreograph a new dance between the branches.
Float petal promises down the river,
sing back the swallows.

Tomorrow the smallest of yards will make space for
   cherry trees.
Their first tears will be painted, each cellular hour
   recorded,
their histories retold.

**Author story note:** *Listening to people talk about holidays they have missed but also how they have enjoyed watching nature; people's hopes that this time of reflection will bring about a greater respect for our natural environment and each other.*

# There is no Future
## Sally Hughes

*1988*

There is no future. There is only today.

I swing back and forth underneath the tree, my scabbed legs gliding out into the soft, empty air. I know this tree well. I rub my cheek against its warm, rough bark, and sit in the smooth bowl where the branches part. In the twist of bare roots underneath, I stir my own marvellous medicine of pond water, grass seed and moss, and then feel guilty, for both my grannies are lovely.

I am allowed as far as the drystone wall at the bottom of the field and the cattle grid on the lane, and I hang around these borders. I never cross the cattle grid – I would be too easily seen – but today I will leap over the tumbledown wall and into the paradise on the other side, where a spring tumbles alongside the old road, and the air is alive with flies and a stench of herbs.

My favourite colour is yellow, for I know that is the true colour of the world. I tell anyone who asks that I want to be a vet when I grow up. They seem to accept this, though I know it is a lie. I will never grow up, for there is only today, and the buzz of the bees, and the songs of birds I don't know the names of, and the deep delicious smell of the earth, so delicious that I cannot resist licking it off my fingers, even though I will probably give myself worms again. My legs swing back and forth, back and forth, forever.

*1996*

The future will come in the year 2000, and everything
will be different and better.

In 2000, I will be 18. I will be done with school. I will
be done with these endless days that are so painful to
live through that I have given up writing a diary, because
the words I write are like dull spoons that cannot
possibly dig out all that is heaped up inside me.

In 2000, nothing will be heaped up – it will all have
melted away, along with my fat. My hair will be long and
straight and I will be as beautiful as my sisters.

The future is a bridge between the dragged-out present
of sweat and chapped thighs and agonising periods and
the golden hours that await me. I do not know where
I will be. I only know I will be elsewhere. The future is
coming for me, and I want to go.

*2006*

As you walk towards me through the pub, your
shoulders are slightly hunched. You are so used to
ceilings being too low for you that you never fully
straighten yourself out. I think, there you are, and after
years of the future being such an unmitigated blank that
I fear it's a sign I will die at an early age, a vista of time
spreads out in front of me.

I can see days spent walking these silver streets and
sitting amongst the deep quiet of books. I can see nights
spent with you.

It is all before us. We have not even touched yet.

## 2013

My future is a person who is here, and not here.

He started in the old year as a cluster of cells, a twitch in my belly like a trapped nerve. Now we are in the hard cold of January, and he has almost arrived. I know everything will change, and I cannot imagine how it will be. I think about what he is and what he will become. Will he be kind, adventurous or clever? Will he be interested in things? Will he know his own mind?

Although we are intertwined, we are separate. Already, he seems to exist because of his own self-will, and not any action of mine. I am certain he hears my thoughts. When I write in my journal he strains a hand or foot against my knicker elastic, as though pressure will convey his feelings. When he grows too quiet I run a shallow bath and throw water over my stomach. He pushes out parts of himself. He is playing with me.

During my nights I fend off spectres of wax-faced dolls that extend stiff, cold fingers toward me. 'You aren't my baby!' I scream. During my days, I am a lumbering bear. I walk the hills of my motherland, waiting, waiting.

## 2020

There is no future. There is only today.

We have fallen out of time. The whirl of washing school uniforms, catching buses and writing to-do lists has stopped. There are only these long hours, in a small house, cupped by hills. The mountains look soft and soothing; they have seen worse than this. We watch the television, and can't make sense of the numbers we read: 10,000; 20,000; 35,000.

We wake with the dawn and sweat around the living room: Burpees! Lunges! Squats! We eat porridge, and try to work. In the afternoon, we move to the garden. It is a wilderness with a purpose of its own. There is a sweet-smelling jungle tangled in the leaves of the cornflowers, and ants march up and down the sticky trunk of the acer tree. I thrust my head into the hedge, trying to find a blackbird's nest. Inside, it is as sinuous and primal as a forest in a fairy tale.

I had thought that in this place I would root myself – stretch out my limbs and burst into blossom. But the future has vanished. I am frightened to think of what is coming, of what we will have lost.

A pair of great tits fly back and forth from the nesting box with dead grass, feathers, a wisp of duckling down blown from the canal. The fresh leaves on the acer unfurl slowly, like tight green fans, and each day they open a little more.

**Author story note:** *Events of recent months and the coronavirus lockdown have prompted me to think about how my conception of the future has shifted and repeated during my life.*

# Now... If I Had a Crystal Ball
**Margaret Bowman**

If I only knew whit lies ahead
I'd ken which path tae take
I'd ayeways hae the upper hand
Wi' choices I'd tae make

So, if I had some inward gist
Oh! now, wouldn't that be jist grand
I'd likely be wan step in front
Aware of whit's been planned

I've tried ma luck wi the 'wise one'
Tellin' fortunes at the fair,
But that wiz jist a waste o' time
Ma mither could tell me mair!

I've looked at what the stars foretell
Tae gie me 'inner sight'
But stars an' planets, an' how they lie
Could not resolve ma plight

I've tried ma hand at gazing balls
That shimmer in the sun
But they can't show what the future holds
Jist ma face... in every one!

But if I knew whit road tae tak
Tae ken jist whaur I'm goin'
Avoiding trouble on the way
By... that would be plain borin'!

So, it's maybe no' such a guid idea
Tae ken how lies yer fate
The path o' destiny twists an' turns
It niver runs oot straight

The meaning o' life and whit's ahead
The truth may be laced wi' sorrow
Its short-lived secret, sour or sweet
Here today and gone tomorrow

So, I'll listen tae some wise old words
That ma Granny used tae tell me
An' there'll be nae need fir a crystal ball, cos
Whit's afore ye'll nae gae past ye!


**Author story note:** *We all would, at one time or another, have thought how handy it would be to know what the future will bring – and many have tried various methods – but in truth we are the masters of our own destiny and it is up to each individual to form their own pathway.*

# Apocalypse Then
## Laura Barbour

Most nights I would position Humphrey the gigantic stuffed hippo behind me; the big spoon, if you will. Once in position, Humphrey morphed into Leonardo DiCaprio and together we drifted into wholesome dreams. In my hormone-ravished mind, those stubby paws easily became strong arms, the nubby ears floppy golden locks, the silence giving way to Hollywood whispers of 'I'll never let go...'. If this were a soft-focus cinematic flashback, Celine would slowly fade in right about now. Oh, those halcyon adolescent years.

It's an absurd scene but, in my defence, the alternative was weirder and even less cool: Maths. On the rare occasion my thoughts were not occupied by my imaginary bedfellow, I would find myself maniacally engaging in the world's worst mental arithmetic task – attempting to count to infinity. Counting sheep and meditation apps got nothing on thirteen-year-old me.

I was only a few years into the religion my mother had chosen for us and I was beginning to struggle to accept that the ultimate goal was to live forever in a utopian society on earth. It was the reason for:

- subservience to men
- not pursuing further education
- modest ear piercings only
- pre-sandwich prayers
- meekness, always.

Following a litany of similar rules would secure the approving nod from God when the ol' fiery End of Times rolled into town, roaring DOWN WITH DISEASE! DESTRUCTION OF SIN! RETURN TO EDEN! The 'good' would skip the line, gaining entry into the hottest post-apocalyptic party in town: Eternal Paradise. Things might have been easier if I hadn't found that prospect fucking terrifying.

My attempts to count to infinity, and find some sense of what my future would be, were hampered by logistics. Part of the deal was that everyone would be forever young, but no further details were available. Would there be an age cap? Would I celebrate 200 years without a wrinkle? The guarantee of perfect health was alluring, but would that mean I would never again know the comfort of Vicks VapoRub? Could I break a bone if I tried hard enough? What would happen if I jumped in front of a speeding lorry?

Can you blame a girl for seeking solace in a hippo?

I only made it six more years. I took my two-tape VHS copy of *Titanic* and got the hell out of there. Tattoos, university and blasphemy followed. I was free! Alive! Vive le revelation!

Except.

As it turns out, God is a lingerer, not so easy to shake from the psyche. And in the deepest crevices of that psyche, a fear took root. On the outside, I was an aloof atheist with cleavage but, beneath that, I was fundamentally terrified of an apocalypse. The apocalypse. Petrified that I would be proved wrong – or right, if I listened to my holy hangover – and there would come an almighty Armageddon where I would be obliterated by hellfire for turning my back on Truth.

I am a very good sleeper. I trained hard for it with

Humphrey in my formative years. And with solid sleep comes a fertile landscape for the subconscious. My dreams are plentiful and epic; vivid all-nighters. In my years as a filthy apostate I have come face to face with God, died many times and have been reunited with childhood best friends whose parents banned them from my influence. Five years ago, at three in the morning, I was bolted into consciousness by the booming arrival of the apocalypse. He was looming over the Earth, bellowing, lightning bolts shooting from fingertips, cracking open the sky, the four horsemen galloping forth to deliver my painful end. The terror was all-consuming as I prepared for judgement. Redundant prayers choked in my throat. Cold sweat was an electric shroud. My body began its collapse into salt. There was no point in resisting.

Kirkcaldy's great thunderstorm of 2015 has a lot to answer for.

My boyfriend leaned out of the window in awe, telling me how cool it was. I tried to breathe and force myself to unlearn, casting out the flawed arguments and vague assertions. The guilt. I knew I had to catch up with logic and reason. I had to forge a new reality.

Soon after, I went to an event where one of my favourite writers read from his new novel. Speaking of his own escape from oppressive religion, he said: 'Real apocalypses are rarely harder than personal ones.' Those words shifted the unwanted, leftover attachments. Those are my holy words. Lord knows I would embroider them on a pillow if I didn't have sausage fingers and impatience in equal measure.

Giving a little bit of faith to those words has made it so clear to me that I can root my convictions in whatever and whomever I choose, with no requirement to narrow my beliefs. It is freeing to believe – and to have the freedom to believe – in:

- the power of my female friendships
- the therapeutic benefits of a sweaty cat wedged in my neck
- the Salem witch who knew about my handwriting
- the gross injustice of Leo's decade-long wait for his Oscar
- the excitement of the unknown.

Before it was okay to read Iain Banks and Stephen King and the ever-Satanic *Harry Potter*, my yellow hardbacked *Children's Bible Stories* painted pictures of forever. Oily, wholesome tableaus of fruit baskets and long skirts and upward smiles. Eternal life in paradise isn't for me. I want nuance and complexity and doses of misery now and then. I love life but I don't want to live forever. I need deadlines! I'd never put in the effort to finally read *War and Peace* or do that skydive or see Alaska if I had forever. The present I have created for myself is full of the peace thirteen-year-old me so badly needed in those past nights with Humphrey and Leo. And it is enough. My future probably isn't infinite and, for that, I thank God.

**Author story note:** *The moment my unconscious, subconscious and conscious were battered together by a thunderstorm in the middle of the night made me realise I had some issues to sort out with God.*

# Ullapool's Sonic Adventure
## Open Book Ullapool

The sound of Beth painting light
Rowers', oars dipping, ferry tooting, wind whistling
The sound of a family fantasising about mountains
Big plastic balls bouncing, Tesco trolleys clattering,
  recycled bottles smashing

The sound of wild swimmers whooping
Cheery hello, a smattering of Gaelic, divining the
  meaning without hearing the words
The sound of deafening pipers in the Macphail
Rain smacking down, gale roaring, chattering at volume

The sound of a quiet little group reading the words in a
  musical way
Men's Shed hammering, it's what they don't say,
  whispering and giggling in the library
The sound of a diesel generator on the Coastguard ship
Seagulls screaming and squawking, endless repetition of
  the same chord,
Harmonising in the Free Church

The sound of the pull of the tide through pebbles
The rush of primary school kids shouting in anticipation
Knowing something good is going to happen
...

Ullapool's Sonic Adventure was written by Barbara,
Madeline, Sandy, Alastair, Ray and Lorraine,
Open Book Ullapool

# Share your love of books...

Scottish Book Trust is an independent national charity.
Our mission is to ensure people living in Scotland have
equal access to books.

If you're enjoying this book, please consider making
a donation so that everyone in Scotland has the
opportunity to improve their life chances through books
and the fundamental skills of reading and writing.

Visit **scottishbooktrust.com/support** to find out
more.

# Remembering
# yesterday

# Back Tae the Future
## Thomas Clark

*Pew! Pew!* The beam o the laser glitters ower ma shouder as ah fling masel tae the grund, imaginin somehow that – this time! – ah'm faster than licht. Ah scurry ahint a barrel o toxic waste and crouch there, the insistent leam o a sniper's tracer pokin for me in the dark, ma Star Wars t-shirt wringin wi sweat.

'Ross?' ah shout. 'Is that you?' Ah ken it must be. He's a wee bit younger than the rest o ma pals, him and his brither, but he's naebody's black sheep. Ah'm no gettin oot o this withoot a fecht. Tae either side, the corridor stretches aff intae a guddle o sichtless possibilities.

Ah lift up ma gun. Its cyclin lichts tell me that ah'm still alive, for noo. But inside is whaur the real battle lies – they say that in *Dune*, ah think, or somethin like it. Ma stomach is heavy wi jelly and ice cream. Ma hert stoonds in ma kist.

The theme frae *Flash Gordon* plays in an endless loop, and for wance it's no jist in ma heid.

'Keysies!' ah shout as ah brek for it, clearin the ramp in three big lowps as c-beams strobe the air. Ah roond the corner, rifle raised, blast anither Space Marine straicht in the back. The lichts gang up jist in time for me tae see her look o disappointment.

'Till deith dae us pairt, eh,' she says, bitterly. She's haudin the gun wrang, and her – *oor* – weddin ring is caught on the trigger.

'Sorry,' ah say. Ah rin ma haun through whit's left o ma hair. It's ma birthday, and ah'm 39 years auld.

We gang oot the airlock, hing up oor guns for noo. Ootside, aneath the green-screen displays and tinfoil-coated pipes and the lifesize model o a Xenomorph (life-size?! Ye ken they're no real, aye?) a wee boy is sittin wi his parents, greetin. He'd burst intae tears at the first sign o this place, this mirkie recreation o the future we'd wance expectit, and has been inconsolable ever since. For the third time that day, we gang up the stairs and leave.

We're ayeweys meanin tae heid somewhaur else, but oor steps keep on leadin us back.

And shuir enough, efter hauf an oor o starin in the windaes o travel agents we're here again, suitin up in the stagin areas o oor suspended animation, buildin dens in stoory air-vents o this museum o oor dreams.

By noo, we've got the hale place tae oorsels. Frae the open airlock we scaitter tae the winds, like bairns frae the soond o a broken greenhoose windae. Ross rins for the craw's nest, the best spot on the map – ah belt it doon the open corridor. Ah ken ah cannae oot-run a laser, but that willnae stop me tryin.

But as ah finally approach the escape velocity o ma wan-time youth, and the muckle 4-0 lours upon the horizon like a speed sign beggin me tae slow doon (or hurry up?), the messy distinctions o space and time brek doon aroond me, aw barriers torn tae targets. It's like the endin o thon film, *2001: A Space Odyssey*, when aw the five dimensions conflate tae the heid o a pin, and everythin that ever wis or will be happens tae ye aw at wance, the complete and utter five-pairt trilogy o yersel. Yer saga has come full circle, or near enough tae it that ye can tell – spoiler alert! – how it's aboot tae end. This is whaur we aw came in.

And yet somethin is still missin frae the story, and it's this. Aw the things ye thocht would happen that never did.

Ah'm no talkin flyin skateboards, here: weel, ah am, but no jist that. Tae be born in Scotland is tae bide wi a sense o yersel as an unwantit interloper in history, the fan-rejected reboot o a franchise that wis fine as it awready wis. Everythin guid has awready happened, and aw that ye're left wi are the references and caw-backs, the selective fetishization o the past as it wis (Han shot first!) and even the present at the instant o becomin the past that Scots has nae better wird yet for than *nostalgia*.

The sentimentalizin o whit wance wis: nostalgia. Like a villain frae a fairy-tale, we disarm it in the namin o it. But we hinnae a wird yet for the idealization o the *future* – or, raither, the future that never happened and, noo, never will. And sae, insteid o safely packin it awa, we're forced tae live it oot, season ticket hauders tae the Never-Never Lands o oor imagination; some hairmless, some... no sae much.

Ah stop. Suddenly, for nae reason at aw that ah can fathom, the lichts on ma kist flash aff, and ma gun lets oot a pitiful whine. Ah'm deid, and ah dinnae even ken why.

It's nae skin aff ma neb, ye ken. Ah'll be back. Jist when awbody has forgotten aw aboot me, ma gun'll switch on and ah'll lowp frae roond a corner, a discordant stab o music, ma ain avengin angel. Hasta la vista, bawheid.

But for noo, ah'm gubbed. Aw ah can dae is wait, and howp that things gang better next time aroond. Ah reach the same junction again, hing a left; there's a noise ahint me, but ah cannae tell whit it means. Whit jist happened.

Birlin, ah hoist ma useless gun, walk backwards intae whitever it is that's there. Jist a cat, ah dout. Or ma ain shaddae, flittin wance mair frae oot ma reach. Twa meenits left tae gang. Ah look doon at the deid display in ma haun and ah pray for the lichts tae cycle, or the music tae fade, or for ony ither reminder that aw this, like everythin else, has awready came tae pass, a lang, lang time ago, in a galaxy faur, faur awa.

# Moon Beams
## Mary Gourlay

'I'm no eating that, I hate mince.' I shout through tae the kitchen whar Mum's dishing up platefuls. I signal ower tae my twin sitting across the table.

'C'mon.'

Wi belt up the stairs twa at a time. The smell o the cooking maks me want tae puke. Joe laughs and says, 'We're no eating it, and that's that.'

I open the linen cupboard door and Joe hoists me up and I land in the pile o blankets on the tap shelf. Joe climbs up ahent me and drags the door shut. It's dark and close in this wee space, safe awa fae the world ootside. Yi could climb up tae the attic fae here and walk alang the beams, but yiv tae be careful no tae put yir foot through tae the room alow.

'She'll no get us in here,' Joe says, then wriggles intae the ither corner and hunkers doon, 'It's a shame though, it's rhubarb crumle and custard fir pudding, mibbee she'll leave us some.'

But I didnae care cos Mum's custard wis aye lumpy.

Dinners wir a battle in oor hoose. Mum wis a terrible cook and if Dad wis hame wi'd hae tae eat it or tak what we'd git, but he's aff golfing wi pals the day. I mind the time he threw a plate at my heed cos I gagged wi the mince in my mooth. I yelled oot that night when the bone comb scraped ower the lump, but I wis stuck in Mum's lap an coudnae git awa.

Joe says, 'We'll sit here till she forgits aboot us, she aye gits mixed up.'

'Hey Midge,' that's his nickname fir me, 'What are yi gonna be when yir big?'

'I dinnae ken.'

'I think yi'll be a ballerina, yir good at that.'

'Mibbee, I kin stand on my taes noo.'

I got ballet pumps fir my birthday. I'd nagged tae git them fir ages, they're red and saft, the best present ever. Lorna Drake fae the 'Princess' comic shows me aw the moves. There's aye a rammy on Saturday mornins when it's pit through the door. Even the laddies want tae read it. I'm definitely gonna be a ballerina.

'What'll yi be?'

'I'm gonna be a fitbaw player fir Celtic and score aw the goals.'

'Bet yi will.'

Joe loved fitbaw, he'd been picked fir the scale team even though we wir only in primary five. Wi played twa touch atween the greenie poles in the back gairden, he aye won, but I wis pretty good tae. The fitbaw pitch wis oor grass and the wuman's next door's tae. Her sons wir aw grown up so they didnae need it. They wir pert o the 'Huns' gang that knocked aboot in the 'Attila Cafe' doon at the shops. It wis scary tae pass them when yi'd been sent fir a message but Joe said they'd niver bather us as wi bided next door tae twa o their leaders, I felt better then.

Dad ran the church fitbaw team and sometimes we'd sneak the real leather baw he brought hame fir dubbing and kick it aboot the backies. It wis sair on yir taes and it didnae help my ballet moves, but it made Joe happy.

I can see him in his fitbaw strip, wee among the ither lads and beaming oot fae the team photo.

'An another thing I want tae dae,' he says, 'I want tae go tae the moon in a rocket, it'd be great.'

I shuffle further doon intae the cushion aneath me.

'It's affy far awa and yi might no git back.'

'Yir just a feardie, Midge, it'd be alright.'

Oor wee brither John wis on the stairs, 'Whar are you twa? Mum wants yi.' He wis a right clype. We didnae let on till it wis safe tae sneak doon, oot the front door and intae the street.

Mince wisnae fir us.

I niver got tae be a ballerina but I wore holes in the shoes practising; instead I got married and had twa bairns, they're aw grown up, and I've a grandson. I show him how tae play twa touch in my wee gairdin, he likes tae win and I like tae let him. Time's past but I can still kick a baw, some things niver leave yi. I wis a social worker fir years, no quite what I wanted tae be, but it paid the bills. Joe didnae git tae play fir his favourite team either, he died in an accident when we wir teenagers. Naebody kent what tae say when it happened and I had a hole in my belly wi aw the greeting. The priest came tae the hoose efter the funeral, there wis drink, sausage rolls and loads o talk aboot nothing. I asked him his name cos I didnae want tae call him 'Father' and Mum wis black affronted. It wis an affy time.

But I like tae think Joe went tae the moon and niver came back, because that's what he wanted.

**Author story note:** *Moonlight drew me back to a time of innocence in my childhood and the story came from there.*

# Future
## Luke Winter

---

IN TIME

Under the great sycamore tree in Berlin, a romance
which had not happened, still did not. The lease was to
end on the apartment that I'd stayed a month in. My
money had run out and here's me not too enthusiastic
to make more from the streets of this city. Stay here? On
the couches of friends – for what? My trip had sought
the glamours of companionship, artistic fraternity,
inspiration, romance. Should I persist to chase tattered
illusions? In Scotland I could return to friends, a cheap
rent, possibilities.

WEIRD

If I only get to tell you one thing, remember this: 'weird'
is an old Scottish word. It can now mean a million
things. Six hundred years ago it meant something only
in Scots. It defined someone who could control the fates.
A 'weird' or 'wyrd' individual could talk with the forces
that wove fortune. The word came into common English
via Shakespeare's witchy Scottish play, and his witches,
the Weird Sisters. Then the word gathered tongues to
become what we mean by it today.

THE WIND SAYS MOVE

There was a big sycamore tree in the courtyard of the
tenement in Berlin. The flat's patio door opened to the
base of it. I stood staring at its leaves that laid slack
against a still summer's day. The leaves drooped like

open palms of green hands. I thought about whether to leave Germany. Without preamble a skirl of wind arrived and blurred the branches of the tree, then left just as quickly. The leaves shoogled back to their stillness. I went back inside and booked a plane. Two days later I was back in Scotland. I went to a festival to work with my friends. A romance with my future girlfriend began that weekend.

## PORTENTS

I have not always believed in portents. Though it is not belief that has brought them to me. Not an idea adopted like that season's fashion, tried with apprehension and found to be acceptable for a while. I believe in portents in the same manner that I believe in friends. The knowledge of who an individual is, and what they bring, happens gradually. Trust is learned. So it has been with portents. A gradual familiarising. So it becomes that one day the wind blows through the trees and you sense a message is being spoken to you.

## FUTURE

In the pub, they each had ideas. Sly or accusatory, doleful and cynically they would roll them out: a parade of potent predictions. Ideas would pour from them, and posture for position as most plausible.

The future happened faster now. These imaginations chattered on a global platform. Predictions became spells that caused an idea to zoom through the present. Predictions gained vitality by virility. The futures that some had come to believe in, began to take place. Global pandemics, new weather, authoritarianism.

# ENLIGHTENMENT

Today we do not talk of the fates. We do not talk of
our part in a wider, wilder world of untameable forces
in such a way. Cleverness has labelled the parts of our
physical reality in an attempt to reduce all objects into
smaller parts. They find the things that make up things,
and give them names. Then find the things that make
up those things, and give them more names. Often the
names that are given are those of the scientist whose
aim was to find something left unlabelled. The result
is that human scientific knowledge reads like a great
school jotter of graffiti tags. Read the names on the
periodic table and the elements of the solar system.
In female anatomy, there is now, and forevermore will
be, the Pouch of Douglas (named by James Douglas, d.
1705).

This attempt to name new parts of reality happened
whilst old voices were silenced. Fate and such
were dismissed by the patriarchal powers of the
Enlightenment as 'old wives' tales'. Those who persisted
in resisting were executed as witches. By silencing the
knowledge of women's voices and weird voices, huge
harm was caused.

Our current vocabulary shies from the unmeasurable.
That which has no mechanical instrument to sing out its
terms is judged silent. The world as we speak of it now is
populated only by measured knowns.

To talk to fate, as the Weird sisters did, was to talk
with something unaccountable. The knowledge of the
Enlightenment did away with the unaccountable, the
folk gods, the superstitions. The enlightened scientists
drove quickly into a single furrow of the darkness,
pulling modern society along behind them. Now we sit
in the dark woods, learning to listen again, learning to
be weird.

# Futures Unforeseen
**Lynn Fraser**

---

I rode your bike in Glasgow's Viccy park. Age 41. A
vintage Raleigh Chopper '69 banana yellow.

A classic. The unmistakable hum of the tyres on the
path. With the wind in my hair, I celebrated you

Drunks on a bench shouted: 'Is that a Chopper? Gonna
gies a shot!' Enchanted and animated they were, as I
whizzed by shouting: 'Aye!' while grinning like a loon.
They cheered, celebrating their past. 'Oh man, I always
wanted wan o' them – gies a backie at least, hen!' I hear
the trail of his voice as he stands and salutes me with his
Carlsberg Special.

Changing gears.

Rainy day in the kitchen at no. 72, years before. It's
bright and hot and the steam runs down the window
as Mammie cooks and complains of bikes in her wee
kitchen, pedals in her sink. There's a familiar aroma of
home-made soup and Brasso as we shine, shine them
mudguards, till they gleam in that warm home light

My wee Chipper bike, and your Chopper. I gaze upon it
with adoration, and a sprinkle of impatience, as it leans
against the kitchen bunker and you run the cloth over
the chain with a look of: 'It's OK, dinnae fret. I'm off to
college soon and this beauty will be yours. And I'll visit!'
You showed me how to polish, you showed me how to
shine. Brother where did you go? Why did you go?

Changing gears.

'Let my blood be a seed of freedom, and the sign that hope will soon be a reality' – Oscar Romero.

I've come to clear your house.

Your bed looks so tiny and abandoned in the room. His photo above it, stuck on with a couple of dods of Blu Tac. A few books, full ashtrays, a lone tooth-brush.

'And where was he, that day, your God!' I shout into the room.

Romero looks sad as I gently take him down off the wall and put him in my pocket.

Where was your God that day? Waiting. Waiting on you arriving.

You so wanted to leave.

Changing gears.

Davey done a cracking job of restoring the bike. We'd taken it out of the skip you'd put it in (why?) and he'd taken it back to Glasgow. Specially ordered new tyres with the classic red line in the middle. Shiny new mudguards, polished seat, the gear-box still perfection and the paintwork touched up. It looked majestic.

After the Chopper's Viccy Park re-birth, Davey asked if it could go on tour to be part of Dundee Rep's stage production of *Sunshine on Leith*.

So, it did. You'd have bloody loved that.

Gently brake... and stop.

**Author story note:** *The future can only be understood in the context of the past. Time dimension stops us from moving backwards or from being still, so we are shoved into it, the future. To move forward we are pushed out of the past which we still take with us, carrying the imprint of its events around with us everyday. We are constantly stepping into the future, while curating the threads to both near and distant history, along the way.*

# Clearing the Fog

**Matthew Keeley**

My future was decided by six words from an English teacher. UCAS applications had leapt upon us weeks earlier like unwelcome visitors and while other Sixth Year pupils invited them in, announcing their grand ambitions and crafting empowering personal statements, I didn't answer the door. My future was still a thick fog in the distance.

Why would I have wanted to think about university before now anyway? University meant student halls with unknown extroverts and unfamiliar lecture halls swarming with alien people who knew more than me and who wouldn't understand my Mariah Carey obsession. Sounded nightmarish.

And what would I even study? A less-than-ten-minutes multiple-choice quiz had helped the school careers advisor decide that I had good people skills.

'Human Resources Management. That would be a good fit for you.'

Had I been channelling someone else? Picking answers at random? People skills? Me? I couldn't even remember the careers advisor's name. I can't remember now if it was a man or a woman. My people skills ended at the edge of my two friends and the idea of speaking to anyone I didn't know was a bizarre and terrifying prospect, like sticking your hand inside a dark box on a TV game show. And what did a Human Resources Manager even do? After shuffling out of the school library, finding a quiet spot in a scabby corridor, and reading a folded-up computer printout, I'd discovered it involved unthinkable acts: recruiting applicants, managing employee wellbeing, appraising staff – all very, you know, people-oriented. My weekend job stacking supermarket shelves and speaking to no one hadn't quite equipped me with the skills for that.

So I abandoned the world of Human Resources almost as quickly as it had been suggested to me – sorry, careers advisor man/woman. Looking to my friends hadn't helped either. Their futures in medicine had been diagnosed years earlier. They'd chosen their subjects around that goal and organised work experience in care homes to implant in their UCAS applications. I'd cancelled my work experience in a solicitor's office – Ally McBeal had made Law seem quirky and colourful – after my induction visit had involved more than three humans and given me a crystal ball glimpse of a claustrophobic future in a drab office.

Deciding on a university course wasn't like anything else at school. No one would tick or cross my answers and there were no solutions at the back of a textbook. At some point in the process I'd pencilled in vague Business courses at a selection of universities – none too far from home. 'Business' could cover lots of things, couldn't it? Shops, factories, advertising firms, uranium mines, snake-petting zoos, Mariah Carey theme parks. So it wasn't really making up my mind at all. It was a kid-on choice.

In Advanced Higher English, I thought I'd be able to forget about university for fifty minutes, plotting out another short story based on some vivid dream I'd had. But even there I couldn't escape the fog that floated closer. My classmates discussed their UCAS choices, boldly naming courses like Environmental Law, Classical

Civilisation, and Art History and Visual Culture, while I bowed my head to my jotter to see if I could crawl between the ruled lines.

'Matthew, what are you applying for?'

Our teacher, Miss Horne, was new to the school that year. She wore trainers some days and had taken us on a theatre trip to see something sexy and confusing. She looked at me from her desk, as if knowing someone needed to ask me.

'Some Business and Management courses,' I muttered, shrugging.

'That's too boring for you.' Another pupil in the class who I'd never spoken to much – surprise, surprise – flicked her hair back with bright fingernails. 'You're too creative. You should do something exciting.'

The compliment felt like a foreign language and made me sit up straighter. I looked to Miss Horne as she nodded, playing with a pen.

'I think you should do English.'

There was probably more to the conversation. She might have told me some of the books she'd read at uni. Might have explained why English was a good choice for me. But all I remember is that sentence because that was all I needed. Those six words were an incantation, breaking a curse and clearing the fog. I didn't need to choose a career. I just needed to choose something I loved. For now. When I told my mum, an English teacher herself, she seemed pleased with my epiphany, probably realising then that I'd end up in teaching too.

Four years later, my siblings handed me graduation cards while Italian guitar music played through speakers and waiters passed menus around. Then, between bobbing helium balloons, Miss Horne appeared, walking into the restaurant like déjà vu and sitting at a table behind me. She didn't spot me and I spent the next couple of hours deciding how to introduce myself and what to call her and whether I should interrupt her before dessert or after she'd asked for the bill. How could I best explain that I had just graduated with an Honours degree from the course she'd told me to apply for? What if she had no idea who I was? Or was annoyed that I'd disturbed her meal with such a pointless anecdote? I realise now, as an English teacher, that a former pupil telling you that you helped make the right decisions about their future will never be a pointless anecdote.

In the end, my worrying became irrelevant. At some point I'd looked up just in time to see the back of her head as she left. My social ineptitude had cost me my chance to say thank you. Good job I hadn't gone into Human Resources Management. The Mariah theme park staff would be a riot. Maybe Miss Horne is reading this now, though. University didn't improve my people skills, but it did help me write stories.

**Author story note:** *I vividly remember my Sixth Year English teacher saying, 'I think you should do English' from behind her desk as the class talked about what university courses we were all applying for. Oddly, no one had suggested it up until then, and I really did make my mind up on the spot when she said it.*

# Share your love of books...

Scottish Book Trust is an independent national charity. Our mission is to ensure people living in Scotland have equal access to books.

If you're enjoying this book, please consider making a donation so that everyone in Scotland has the opportunity to improve their life chances through books and the fundamental skills of reading and writing.

Visit **scottishbooktrust.com/support** to find out more.

# Changing tomorrow

# Reasons to be Cheerful
## Abir Mukherjee

'When did the future switch from being a promise to a threat?'

So goes a line from Chuck Palahniuk's novel *Invisible Monsters*, and these days it's a fair question.

Yet the future has always been tinged with frissons of fear: of change; of the different; of the unknown, but recently our fears appear to have multiplied. The world seems less safe, less certain than it has been in most people's lifetimes, rocked almost daily by factors as daunting and disparate as demagogic populists, climate change and global pandemics.

And on a personal level there's the inescapable fact of time itself. I'm getting older, reaching that stage in life where everything seems to be that little bit harder. The joints creak a bit more, the pounds don't seem to shift as easily and the small print looks ever smaller. It's hard not to equate this decline with a more general feeling that the whole world is going downhill, and suddenly I find myself uttering that rallying cry of the old – *things were better in my day*.

But here's the rub. In many ways, and for many people around the globe, things are better today than they've ever been. Over the last few decades, millions have been pulled out of absolute poverty and have seen their lifespans and life chances improve. That is surely grounds for hope, and much of that hope is down to advances in science and technology.

The sad fact is that I'm an optimist, and that optimism

is rooted in a belief in the fundamental goodness of people. Wherever I go in the world, what always strikes me is just how similar most people really are. Regardless of race or creed, we all have the same needs, the same basic desires for the future and for our children's future.

We live in a world of connectivity, a world which even two decades ago would have been unthinkable. Information, they say, is power, and every day, thousands more people gain that power, accessing knowledge and information which can transform their lives. Be it ever cheaper smartphones allowing farmers in remote parts of the globe to find out the prices of their goods without making a day's trek to market, or high quality education being delivered online to rural areas or locked down towns and cities, technology has the power to improve all our lives.

But technology is a double-edged sword. It has made our world smaller than ever before. The technology that allows us to be in Tokyo for breakfast, London for lunch and New York for supper also allows once localised viruses to spread quickly across the globe. And while today, in the midst of world-spanning pandemic, it might be hard to appreciate the strides we've made in combating diseases which have plagued us for millennia, the speed at which scientists are responding to ever-evolving challenges is breathtaking.

And then there's social media – Twitter, Facebook, WhatsApp and the like – which though often the bane of life, have transformed political and social discourse. For the first time in history, these platforms have given a voice to those who've never had one. They've given protest movements the ability to organise and highlight the everyday injustices which face so many of us. Without them, I wonder if movements for democracy or campaigns such as Black Lives Matter would ever gain traction. Of course, these platforms also polarise opinion and are also utilised by the unscrupulous: the trolls and the malevolent state actors, ever eager to undermine. We need to be wary of this and figure out how to harness the good without becoming hostage to the bad.

Progress and change always come with downsides and dangers. My hope is that we will remember our better natures, and make use of new technologies to empower those who have been marginalised, to raise ever greater numbers of people out of poverty and to help heal some of the damage done to the planet. Indeed I'm confident that we shall do so. Sometimes, amidst the noise and the spectacle of our interconnected, unsleeping and televised world, it's difficult to have much confidence in the future. But the future is what we make it, and I believe there is enough that is noble in the human spirit for us to look to tomorrow with hope.

I'll end with the words of my hero, Mahatma Gandhi. 'The future depends on what you do today.'

What will you do today to create that future?

# The Future is Queer

**AJ Clay**

The future is a question mark
It's 'other', 'decline to answer'
Walks the line between pink and blue
Raises eyebrows in changing rooms

The future is terrifying
It hates outsiders, crushes difference
Steals away hard-won freedoms
Keeps the closet doors locked

The future is exciting
It's a blank page, waiting to be filled
With rough drafts, slow revisions,
First steps along an unknown path

The future is queer
It comes in, striding confidently
In battered DMs, draped in flags
Defiant, head held high in the parade

The future is unknown
But it's rainbow-bright
And it's ours.

# For the Moment
**Robbie Handy**

Early in the April mornin Ah hear the kraawk o craws, the kroo-kroo o doos an countless call and response chirps an cheeps o unknown provenance.

Ah keek through ma windae at the Glen oer the road an seagulls stalk the grass by the bairns' playpark as the trees stand still an the traffic light at the crossin shines green.

Ah'm aye up early for work (and mair grateful than ever Ah can graft at aw the noo), but afore Ah turn on the breakfast telly news Ah've started listenin tae the birds.

Ah'm feart. When Ah think o the future, Ah cannae see past the next few days or weeks. Ma only real ambition right noo is tae make it through this crisis wi me an ma faimly an pals alive an intact.

When Ah listen tae the birds, when Ah really listen, it makes me feel mair calm for a wee while. Ah mind that, in the midst o chaos, there's still some sort o natural rhythm an order. An at a time when Ah see few fellow humans outwith a phone screen or telly, it minds me there's probably someone else next door or alang the street listenin tae the same dawn chorus, an probably steelin themselves for an everyday battle much bigger than ma ain.

An then Ah mind how lucky Ah am. An Ah feel ashamed for feelin feart an bein selfish. An Ah start tae think what Ah'd like the future tae feel like once, God willin, we get through this.

This thing is indiscriminate, but if ye dinnae have the wherewithal tae isolate in comfort an ye've tae walk or tak buses cos ye dinnae have a car, an ye've tae share the place ye live wi a wheen o other folk, ye're no as protected as those who are sittin pretty. Yet ye might be leavin yer cramped hoose every day an kissing yer bairns bye and settin off tae work in a hospital tae put yer life on the line tae save us aw.

So in the future it would be braw if the first were last and the last were first – if we looked at a nurse or a shop assistant wi the same awe an admiration that's usually reserved for someone who happens to have made a lot of money, but hasnae done much else tae make things better for everyone. But oor admiration should extend tae paying these folk much mair too – kind words dinnae fill bellies or pay rents an mortgages. Let's dae a bit o wealth redistribution in the future, it's aboot time.

It would be guid if, in the future, we mind that when the country shut doon, it happened cos the ordinary workers couldnae keep at their daily grind. An we should mind that captains o industry who inherited their positions were locked in their hames helpless, together alone with the rest of us. And that it turns oot even those self-proclaimed, self-made men an women we love tae lionize werenae quite as self-sufficient efter aw – a load o folk has been helpin them the hale time. In the future, it should be all o us first. Naebody should be judged better than anybody else.

An Ah hope we mind that we're aw Jock Tamson's bairns in the future, an that in hospitals across the country in these hard days, medics o aw creeds, colours an religions were savin oor lives an sacrificing theirs, bravely steppin intae the breach as if their PPE was armour rather than plastic and paper. In the future, we shouldnae look for scapegoats an there should be mair checks an balances tae stop poisonous ideas driftin unchallenged through corridors of power – an takin life as ignorance licensed by law.

Ah hope that in the future we're much kinder tae each other an tae oor planet. That we continue spraffin tae neighbours an sparin them a few minutes of oor time, oor precious time that we noo realise isnae precious because we should be spending every wakin minute o it making money and paying bills and buying things. Naw – it's precious cos we never ken when it'll run oot like sand atween oor fingers. So oor last words tae someone should be somethin warm an lovin rather than cauld an callous.

We will have a perty, in the future, when this is officially over. But Ah hope we caw canny an keep the collective heid, because too many o us will be mournin those we've lost, who we never got a chance tae say bye tae properly. So celebrate aye – cos life is a gift tae gie thanks for – but mind that there will be deep wounds tae heal.

An when we buy oor cairry oots for that perty in the future, when it's aw over, Ah hope we look the checkout assistant behind the plastic screen in the eyes and say 'thank you' an mean it fae the bottom o oor hairts. An that we tidy up efter oorselves and dinnae dare complain aboot recyclin oor rubbish intae multi-coloured cooncil bins in the mornin. Then Ah hope we aw sober up for a guid lang while.

Ah hope Ah listen tae ma ain advice an that this is a hard lesson, but one that lasts a decent lifetime.

This might be the sairest fecht we ever face thegether an wha really kens what the future holds?

Aw Ah ken is that, right noo, they birds are still singin an that light's still green.

That this is life.

For the moment.

**Author story note:** *Lookin oot ma windae this mornin an wonderin what the future holds when the world seems tae be fallin apart.*

# Sùil Air Adhart
## Cairistìona Stone

Ghabh mi cuairt o chionn ghoirid, 's mi a' beachdachadh
air an àm ri teachd – mo smuaintean a' falbh eadar dè
a tha romhainn sa bhliadhna 2020 's nas fhaide air
adhart agus dè a bhios ag atharrachadh dhuinn' – cho
fada 's a chì sinn. Cuspair gu math leathann, farsaing,
inntinneach.

Gu cinnteach, tha tionndaidhean ùra mar coinneamh
mar dhùthaich, mar rìoghachd – nithean a bha aig aon
àm cho cunbhalach ri plosgadh cridhe rèidh 's a tha a-nis
bun-os-cionn, an snaidhm air ceann an t-snàithlein air
fuasgladh, gun chothrom a cheangal air ais mar a bha o
thùs.

Cho ùr 's a tha Brfhàgail, tha sinn' ann an staid a
tha caran cugallach. Air dhuinn bliadhnaichean a
chaitheamh a strì mu thimcheall Breatamach, tha sin
a-nis air ar cùlaibh. Abair cath a lean ùine... an iomairt
Fàgamaid a' coiteachadh airson Sasamach agus an
iomairt Fuiricheamaid a' strì gu daingeann na aghaidh.
Mar thoradh, tha còmhraidhean agus strì air togail
ceann a-rithist a thaobh an dara reifreann mar dhòigh
air briseadh air falbh bhon Rìoghachd Aonaichte.
Chaidh Achd Reifreann Neo-eisimeileachd na h-Alba a'
stèidheachadh ann an 2013 ach, anns na taghaidhean
a lean ann an 2014, cha d' fhuaras bhòtaichean gu
leòr airson neo-eisimeileachd – ged nach robh na
h-àireamhan ro fhada bho chèile. A' coimhead air adhart,
saoil am bi reifreann ùr ann? Ma bhitheas... dè an toradh
's a' bhuil a bhios ann airson Alba? 'S e tìde a dh'innseas!

An dràsta fhèin, tha Prìomh Mhinistear na h-Alba
(ceannard a' Phàrtaidh Nàiseanta) a' sireadh an dara
reifreann – 's na h-aghaidh, tha Prìomh Mhinistear na
Rìoghachd Aonaichte a' diùltadh. Chan e gu bheil Alba
mar aon a' seasamh còmhla rithe... buidheann le miann
briseadh air falbh – buidheann a' miannachadh aonachd.

Air dhomh an earrann seo a thoirt gu crìch, 's mi air
snìomh ri chèile faclan neo-àbhaisteach, tha e a' bualadh
orm gu làidir gur e gnàthasan-cainnte ùr-nòsach a
tha mi a' cleachdadh a-nis. Nach iongantach mar a
ghluaiseas cànan ann an leudachd agus farsaingeachd
airson briathran 's abairtean gu tur às ùr a chruthachadh
co-cheangailte ri staid chaochlaideach an t-saoghail. San
àm ri teachd, an dùil nach bi faclan às ùr againn nach eil
againn an-dràsta? Saoilidh mi gu bheil sin gun cheist.

A' toirt sùil air ais air a' chuairt ud air na thog mi dealbh
aig toiseach a' phìos sgrìobhaidh seo, tha mi nam shuidhe
air gainmheach ghlan, gheal, 's a' togail cnap nam làimh,
mar shìoda grinn. Tha mi mothachail gu bheil gach
gràinnean a' dòrtadh trom mheòirean gu luath – a' cur
nam chuimhne mar a tha an saoghal fhèin a' sìoladh às
le cabhaig. Tha mi a' faicinn fada bhuam na creagan air
taobh thall na tràghad. Nas fhaisge, tha mo shùilean a'
toirt a-steach nan sualaichean a' briseadh air a' chladach
– na h-eich bhàna neo-thròcaireach a' dèanamh air druim
na tràghad mar airm aonaichte, neo-gheamanta. Os mo
chionn, tha mo chluasan a' tighinn beò ri ceòl na h-eòin
mara – an t-uabhas dhiubh, 's iad ag èirigh 's a' tuiteam air
osag ghaoithe. Fada a-mach, tha na sùlairean a' bualadh
air a mhuir 's a' togail ceist eile nam inntinn... an dùil
am bi na Nisich a' dol a Shùlaisgeir gu bràth tuilleadh?
Às bith am bi no nach bi, tha aon nì gu cinnteach – às
bith dè a tha romhainn – seasaidh creagan, tràigh, fairge,

tonnan, gainmheach, eòin agus gach gnè de nàdar buan, cho maireann ris a' ghrèin. San àm ri teachd, cha tig atharrachadh air na nithean sin a tha nam lèirsinn – ged a thig tionndadh air iomadach nì eile.

Le sùil air adhart, 's e prosbaig gu math mì-shoilleir, eu-cinnteach a tha toirt dhuinn beachd air dè a dh'fhaodadh nochdadh san àm ri teachd. Chan eil e furasta idir corrag a chur gu misneachail aon taobh no taobh eile – a-màireach a bha mì-chinnteach nuair a b' fheàrr e gar cumail fo smachd 's a' diùltadh stiùir no comhair a thoirt dhuinn. Leis mar a tha an saoghal a' dol, saoilidh sinn nach tig deireadh air a' bhochdainn, air tinneas, cogadh, aimhreit no air na mòr-thubaistean de gach seòrs' a tha gar cuairteachadh aig an àm. Dhuinn uile, mar dhaoine beò sa bhliadhna 2020, tha ceistean leatromach mun cuairt a tha gun fuasgladh... làn-bhuil blàthachadh na cruinne, tanachadh filleadh òsoin, an astar aig a bheil cip-dheighe a leaghadh, mar a tha teinntean gun chrìoch a' slugadh suas Coille-uisge an Amasoin, 'sgamhain an t-saoghail'. 'S chan eil an sin ach beagan eisimpleirean à duilgheadasan gun àireamh. An dùil an tig piseach air na suidheachaidhean sin – gu h-àraid nuair a tha uiread thar ar smachd?

Ach, chan fheum sinn' a bhith dubhach! Tha uimhir mun cuairt a tha brosnachail, gealltanach, dòchasach a thaobh na dh' fhaodar siubhal maille rinn gus an àm ri teachd.

Chuala mi o chionn ghoirid, fear a' dèanamh òraid aig na 'Osgaran' agus abair thusa gun tug na briathran aige togail dhomh. Fhad 's a bha e a' còmhradh, bhuail e orm gun robh làn-thuigse aige air na nithean a tha luachmhor an-dràsta fhèin – 's a bhios luachmhor a' gluasad air adhart. An ann air beartas a bha e a' bruidhinn? No iomraiteachd? An e àrd-chliù, no soirbheas? 'S dòcha fèillmhorachd no moit? Dh' fhaodadh e a bhith air an cothrom sin a ghabhail ach ghabh esan slighe eile – amasan gu math nas prìseile aige san amhairc – neamhnaidean airidh air an roinn a-mach. Ghlac e an cothrom airson an sgaoileadh nar measg uile, seudan ris am bu chòir dhuinne greimeachadh le gach lùths, nithean a tha uasal, ionmholta, brosnachail. Dh'ainmich esan ceartas, còraichean, co-ionnanachd, gràdh, truas, neo-fhèinealachd, maitheanas, taic, foghlam, treòrachadh, an dara cothrom, saorsa, teasairginn, sìth. Cò nach iarradh gum biodh na luachan sin againn uile leis gach ceum a nì sinn mu choinneamh an t-àm ri teachd. Deagh-mhisneachail, a' glèidheadh dòigh-smuaineachadh deimhinneach, nach gabh sinn ceum làidir, dòchasach air adhart, còmhla.

Cha robh latha gun dà latha – an saoghal buailteach do chaochladh, le atharrachadh de gach seòrs san t-sealladh ach a dh' aindeoin sin, faodaidh sinn làrach-coise do-àicheadh fhàgail aig an àl ri teachd mar shamhla air na nithean a mhaireas nuair a thèid gach nì eile a' sguabadh air falbh.

# Looking Forward

A short while ago I went for a walk, and I thought about the future – my thoughts ranging from what lies before us in 2020 to further ahead and what will change for us – as far as we can see. A broad, deep subject, and an interesting one.

There are certainly new things in store for us as a country, as a kingdom – things that were once as regular as a steady heartbeat are now turned upside down, the knot that held the threads together undone, with no chance of tying it together as it once was.

Brexit is the new reality, but it leaves us in an uncertain state. We have spent years campaigning about whether Britain should leave, and we had another long battle before that... the Leave campaign lobbying to separate from the UK and the Remain campaign fighting relentlessly against it. As a result, the discussions and campaigns are now raising their heads again in a debate about a second referendum as a way of breaking away from the United Kingdom. The Scottish Referendum Act was passed in 2013, but in the votes that followed not enough ballots were cast to achieve independence – although the numbers were close. Looking ahead, is it likely there will be a new referendum? If there is... what result and what impact will it have on Scotland? Only time will tell! Right now, the First Minister of Scotland (head of the Scottish National Party) is calling for a second referendum – and opposing her is the Prime Minister of the United Kingdom, who will not allow it. It's not as if Scotland is standing together united... one group wants to break away – one group wants union.

Writing that passage involved weaving together some unusual words, and it strikes me that I'm using newly coined phrases now. Language shifts in surprising ways, expanding to include brand new words and phrases to describe our changing world. In future, will there be new words we don't have right now? I think that is beyond question.

Looking back to that walk that I mentioned at the start of this article, I'm standing on a clean, white beach, lifting a handful of sand, like fine silk. I notice how each grain of sand runs quickly through my fingers – reminding me how swiftly the world turns. In the distance, I see the cliffs at the other end of the beach. Closer to me, I take in the waves breaking on the beach – the restless white horses galloping towards the shoreline like an army marching single-mindedly. Above me, my ears are assailed by the music of the seabirds – multitudes of them, rising and falling on the breeze. Far out, the gannets are diving into the sea, prompting me to wonder... will the men of Ness ever go to Sula Sgeir again? Whether they will or won't, one thing is certain – whatever lies ahead of us – the cliffs, beach, ocean, waves, sand, birds and nature in all its forms will endure, as eternal as the sun.

In future, those things that I can see now will not change – though many other things may be transformed.

Looking forward, it is through an unclear and unreliable lens that we look to form our views on what might appear in future. It is by no means easy to put one's finger on something with confidence and make a prediction – the uncertainty of tomorrow constrains us, refusing to help or guide us. The way the world is going, we cannot see an end to poverty, sickness, war, discord or the great calamities of all kinds that surround us at this time. For all of us who are alive in 2020, there are weighty questions with no apparent answers... the full impact of global warming; the thinning of the ozone layer, the speed with which the ice caps are melting, how wildfires are engulfing the Amazonian rainforests, 'the lungs of the world'. And those are only a few of the innumerable examples. Can we expect to see any improvement in this situation – especially when so much is beyond our control?

But we shouldn't be despondent! There is so much happening that is encouraging, promising and hopeful for us to take forward into the future.

A short while ago I heard a man making a speech at the Oscars, and I must say his words made an impression on me. As he was talking, it struck me that he fully understood what is really important right now – and what will be important as we move forward. Was he talking about wealth? Or celebrity? Or fame, or success? He could have taken the opportunity to talk about those things, but he took a different direction – he had far more precious ambitions in mind – offering up pearls of wisdom. He seized the opportunity to scatter them in our midst, jewels that we should try to grab with all our might, things that are noble, laudable, encouraging. He spoke of justice, rights, equality, love, compassion, selflessness, forgiveness, support, education, leadership, second chances, freedom, relief, peace. Who would not want to be mindful of those virtues with every step we take into the future! Confident, maintaining a positive frame of mind, let us take each strong, hopeful step forward, together.

There was never a day without its setbacks – the world is liable to be unreliable, with all kinds of change happening even as we look, but despite that we can leave clear footprints for the coming generations to follow, as an example of the things that endure when everything else is swept away.

# Past, Present and Future
## Dean Atta

Remember when your ex-boyfriend asked you to pay him back because he bought a drink for your friend? Remember how uncomfortable that request made you feel? Why would it be your responsibility to pay him back?

You grew up poor. The child of a single mother. Neither your father nor your sister's father paid child maintenance. Your mother was hard working and proud. She didn't have debts or credit cards. She lived within her means. Most of your friends' parents were poor, too. You were okay with being poor. You understood you were poor way before you understood you were Black or gay.

Among your friends, whoever had money would somehow share it. Nothing extravagant. Walking around Portobello Road Market. Just looking, mostly, but sometimes finding something you could afford. If you couldn't afford it your friend might give you the money, and vice versa. No one ever kept a tally of who owed who. You owed each other everything. You confided in each other when things were tougher than usual. This was your idea of friendship.

You formed close bonds with other working class students who hadn't taken a gap year and didn't have financial support from family. People who had to take out student loans and take part time jobs to see them through university. When you ran out of food, you had friends who would feed you. Often, when you were running low, you would ring around and see what each other had. Coming together with ingredients for a communal meal. You remember: a sweet potato, an onion, a pepper, rice, half a block of cheddar cheese, and some spices.

After university, you moved back to Mum's, and you stayed there for much longer than either of you had expected. Sometimes you paid rent, mostly you didn't. Your mum trusted you to help out when you could afford to. However, she didn't rely on you for money, like many of your friends' parents did. She had been promoted several times at work over the years and was no longer just making ends meet. She could afford a mortgage and had utilised her 'right to buy' her council home.

You were pursuing a career as a freelance poet. You didn't have a clue how this was going to make you money. This made mum nervous but she never discouraged you. She celebrated your every performance, radio and TV appearance, and everything you had published. Other relatives asked if and how much you were being paid but Mum simply wanted to know if you were happy.

You were happy, mostly, but you found it hard to talk about money. Eventually, you were being paid for poetry commissions and performances, and to deliver poetry workshops. You had many friends who were poets and you noticed many of them found it hard to talk about money, too. You would buy each other drinks and never kept a tally. However, when you were booked to perform at the same event, you wondered whether you were all being paid the same amount. You suspected not.

You started talking about money with your poet friends. You found out that fees for commissions and events could be negotiated, you didn't have to say 'yes' to what you were offered. You started negotiating and telling your friends to do the same. Some of them made excuses about why they didn't want to: they didn't have as much experience as you, they didn't have as big a social media following, etc.

You met that ex-boyfriend. He had moved to London from Australia and had no family or safety net in the UK. He was drinking in Soho members bars whilst trying to save for a mortgage. He wasn't living within his means. This meant he kept a tally of everything he felt was owed to him. You understood his reasons but it didn't fit your idea of a relationship, at the time.

Your current relationship took you all the way to Scotland. You met him in London but he got a job in a hospital near Glasgow, and you followed him there. When he suggests you use an app to keep a tally of your shared household expenses, you agree that it's a good idea.

Your career is going well. You've published a novel about a poor Black boy, much like yourself. Your book wins an award and is shortlisted for many others. Everything is changing.

You have an agent now, and it's her job to negotiate money on your behalf. A hashtag on Twitter, #PublishingPaidMe, reveals how much more white authors get paid compared to authors of colour. Amidst a global pandemic, you attend a meeting on Zoom to discuss this with other Black writers. You see Benjamin Zephaniah and Malorie Blackman on the call and think, 'This is epic.' Many other Black writer friends call you to discuss your experiences with your publisher, tell you about their experiences with other publishers, and ask advice about advances and royalties. You are much more comfortable talking about money now.

You think of that ex and how he finally did afford a mortgage in London. 'Good for him,' you think. You're happier than ever living in Glasgow. You miss your family and friends in London but you're making new pals here. You join the Scottish BAME Writers Network and feel part of a community. You have many hopes for the future.

You hope working class children do not feel discouraged from following a career in the arts. You hope the arts survive the pandemic. You hope those who have 'made it' talk about how it happened for them. You hope emerging artists are not exploited depending on their ability or confidence to negotiate for higher fees. You hope agents sign up more Black writers, so publishers can no longer say they don't know where to find us. You hope publishers value us for our stories and don't devalue us because of the colour of our skin.

# Share your love of books...

Scottish Book Trust is an independent national charity. Our mission is to ensure people living in Scotland have equal access to books.

If you're enjoying this book, please consider making a donation so that everyone in Scotland has the opportunity to improve their life chances through books and the fundamental skills of reading and writing.

Visit **scottishbooktrust.com/support** to find out more.

# Lockdown reflections

# Daughter
## Hamish Hutchinson

I look into your eyes and see an astronaut,
Commence countdown, engines on,
Shaping constellations in your own universe,
Floating across the new frontier.

I look into your eyes and see a pirate,
Raise the sails and chart your course,
Australia your destination, your journey unfolds,
High seas on higher hopes.

I look into your eyes and see an artist,
Your mind a canvas,
Splashing colour, drawing on dreams,
The mess is amazing.

I look into your eyes and see a teacher,
Every day an education,
Your brother your classroom,
Your subjects; new tricks and bad habits.

I look into your eyes and see a storyteller,
Once upon a time or galaxies afar,
Heroine, adventurer, comedian, writer,
Every end a new beginning.

I look into your eyes and see the future.

**Author story note:** *I was home schooling my daughter during lockdown and it was fantastic to see her enthusiasm for so many different subjects, from NASA activities to 'pirate day' and, of course, countless stories. It made me wonder at her future and how she will look back at this time. I wanted to capture this moment of her life for her.*

# To Hold and be Held
**Rachel Alexander**

---

I'm not sure I can remember the last time I hugged
my mum, but I remember clearly the last time I didn't
hug her. We met in the street: out in the open and at a
distance from each other. She'd driven over with wee
jammy cakes for me and the boys and we staged an
odd pantomime of a handover. She stepped forward
and I stepped back. She put the tupperware on the
ground and withdrew. There was an odd and fleeting
moment of connection as I picked up the box she'd been
holding until moments before. An inadequate, hollow
connection.

When mum was ill, I reached for her hand and stroked
it. With an oxygen mask and hooked up to machines, I
couldn't hug her then either. I could sit with her though,
next to her. Her hand was heavy and slightly limp. As I
traced the veins on the back of her hand, I realised how
familiar it was to me. I knew those hands. I know them;
their strength and their skill.

When I was wee, Mum would stroke the bridge of my
nose if I was ill or couldn't sleep. The warm pressure
of her hand meant I knew I wasn't alone. In a busy
household, this was time devoted purely to me and
I loved it. I felt important and I felt cherished. Held.
Letting someone know that you're there is a simple but
precious gift. I was given it freely and now pass it on.

After the operation, I moved in to help care for her.
An odd part of me looked forward to offering her some
of the comfort that she had shared with me and others

for years. Mum was always the first to offer practical and emotional support and I readied myself to step successfully into that role for her. Yet she cried as I directed the shower spray at her altered body. It had to be done, but she flinched at my touch. Exhausted and disorientated from the lingering anaesthesia, she recoiled and shouted for my dad. It felt awful that my touch wasn't a comfort, that I was causing her pain and distress.

Her hands have always been busy and full, never still. Everything Mum tackles, she does so with enthusiasm and zeal. She makes things; paints, sews, crochets, weaves. When we were wee, she made playsuits for me and my sister. I remember being allowed to choose the material, giggling as her arms circled me with a cold tape that made me squeal as it brushed against my wee belly.

Standing two metres apart on an empty pavement, there was a moment when we looked at each other and I felt the warmth from her. Not a hug, not yet.

# After Weeks of Working at a Hospital in Stockport

**Romalyn Ante**

---

'Health experts have warned that the virus can live
on the soles of footwear for five days.' – Daily Record

Mother comes home for her quarantine
birthday, leaving her surgical shoes by the doorstep.

In the exhausted light of an extractor hood,
purple yam balls boil in coconut cream.

The aroma salves a certain ache
in the hamstrings of the wind.

Mother's hands are sandpaper rough,
each digit, a crack of joints.

But Mother's eyes illume – in the blooms
of candlelight and yellow balloons.

Will tomorrow be bright as our songs
that lift the roof and thrill the marigolds?

Will tomorrow not interrupt? Like Mother's bleep
that propels her out – a lone shoe on the boot scraper.

The street delinquents have come again
and flung the other one to that septic sky.

Will tomorrow be like Mother's laughter? Sunset-
glazed. Only the shadows of crows graze her face.

# For Hope
**Susan Gray**

The virus comes stalking
in the grey March mist –
Hunkered in our homes
we watch its fingers spread
and hope our barricades
of toilet rolls and tins
will keep us safe.
We are self isolating,
social distancing,
banished by fear
from fellow humans,
while flickering screens
bring portents of doom
to every home.
And yet – taking a walk –
Government authorised –
I hear new lambs
bleating by the Mill,
and far away,
in a city to the west,
there is a baby's cry –
the start of a family's new generation
has arrived – and her name
is Hope.

...

For a baby girl, born March 2020,
In Queen Elizabeth Hospital, Glasgow.

**Author story note:** *The start of lockdown, sitting at home feeling depressed, my cousin calls to say the first of the new generation has been born in our family – and things didn't seem too bad after all.*

# Je Vais
## Lily Raper

Future. At my age, it's supposed to be a happy word, full
of opportunity and potential, stretching out in front of
me like a yellow-brick road leading towards a glittering
Happily Ever After. Career, mortgage, family, kids, the
perfect suburban dream.

The word 'future' no longer carries the associations it
once did. It's a strange time to be graduating, just as it's
a strange time to be doing just about anything. Eating,
working, living, breathing, all done with that heavy
black cloud hanging overhead, future. Every day the
word sounds more like a threat.

My last exam was a French oral. I was asked questions
about feminism, the film industry, art and culture
through the safety net of my computer screen. And,
finally, more of a parting query than a real interrogation:
what are your plans for after graduation? I got as far as
'je vais' before realising that I no longer had an ending
for the sentence in any language. In a few short months,
all my plans had been obliterated as the pandemic blew
the working world apart.

What will the commencement speech they give at my
webcam graduation sound like? These kinds of events
are supposed to be uplifting, encouraging us to soar
to new heights, seize tomorrow today, and whatever
else they found on inspirationalquotes.com. Perhaps
they'll replace their generic platitudes with honest
disclaimers: your career is not guaranteed; your health
is not guaranteed; your civil rights are not guaranteed;

your planet's health is not guaranteed; your future is not guaranteed. None of this would be news, of course, but at least we wouldn't be pretending otherwise. The billboard advertising green pastures and white-picket fences rings false in the face of the four-lane pileup below.

Graduation used to be a summit; now it looks more like a cliff edge. I studied French for five years, thinking of careers in teaching, translation, tourism. I've arrived at the peak just in time to watch borders slam shut in my face, and at my back lies the devastation of a global pandemic. I live in one of the most developed nations in the world – I'm one of the lucky ones. My parents and I drag kitchen furniture out onto the driveway and sunbathe while cyclists and dog walkers pass at a two-meter distance. We must look like a postcard of lockdown privilege.

The sunniest Spring on record, the news said today. They placed the item at the end of the broadcast in the slot where they usually have a fluff piece to detract from the wall-to-wall horror preceding it. Forty thousand dead, peaceful protestors beaten and gassed, but at least it's sunny. Taps aff, yippee.

It's a delightful reminder of the backburner cataclysm waiting for us on the other side of the mass graves. How many years left before we burn? Sixty? Forty? Twenty? Never enough, no matter how much optimism I can dredge up to face off against the onslaught of science.

In my day, we expected a nuclear apocalypse, mum tells me. We all thought the end of the world was coming at the push of a button. Will the world end with a bang? A whimper? A Tweet? This cliff edge is beginning to feel like a knife edge. How do I plan for a future that could be blown apart at any moment? How does Generation

Discontent cope with broken promise after broken promise? How do I write a story about Schrodinger's future? How do I plan for a life that is falling apart?

The answer is that I don't plan. I write. I write and write and write in the hope that it gets me somewhere before time runs out. The yellow brick road holds nothing but broken promises and empty gestures. There will be no Happily Ever After at its end. I can only make my own path, and hope.

**Author story note:** *My story was inspired by my French oral examiners who, at the end of the exam, asked what my plans were after graduation. It was the most difficult question they asked me, not because of the language barrier, but because my exam was taking place at the height of pandemic chaos, and I no longer knew what my future would hold.*

# Through the Window
## Polly Pomeransky

I paint, you know.
Not very well, but it helps pass the time.
I write too.
Used to write about my 30 years
Mainly housebound – and the suffering.
Everybody suffers.
The dreams I had yesterday have long past,
As I sit looking out the window;
Through the glass.

Lockdown means nothing to me
Just my normal way of life.
As I sit looking out the window
Through the glass;
And see Arthur's Seat.
Interrupting sunrises and sunsets,
Colours so bright.
An artist's palette of rainbows
Fading into night.
Beauty and colour dependent on my eye.
On the sun.
On the One.
Don't let me die.

The other window, a view of the castle
Brimming with history
Fireworks and fairy tales;
And so much mystery.
Watching for the knight to raise his sword over Calton Hill

To gallop here to my ivory tower on his horse.
A philosopher never tires of –
The Athens of the North.

And when the watching and waiting end,
I'll return to the city,
To my future.
Racing there in my wheelchair, without a care.
Painting and writing and laughing again
Breathing in the fresh air;
I'll thrive
In Eden.
Freedom.
I am alive.

# Future
## Claire Poole

---

'Okay, Arianna, stay safe until we link again next week. Bye.' I watch the young woman's image fade and say 'Off' to shut down the wall. Unusual, I know, as most people leave it on all the time, but I am old-fashioned enough to like some down time. I stretch, roll my shoulders and rub my eyes. I'm tired, very tired, and wonder again whether it might be time to finally retire. I am 90 after all, and although I have been online counselling since the First World Lockdown of 2020, I secretly admit that I preferred the old way when psychotherapist (me) and client communicated face to face, in the same room. Of course that wasn't possible during the 2020 lockdown so we all switched to teletherapy. After some time, people realised that there were issues with such work. Micro facial expressions are missed, and tone of voice is less clear, so reading emotions was more difficult – until some bright spark came up with the software to read these cues.

Nowadays I have a continuous ticker-tape strip at the bottom of my screen saying 'anxious…irritated…sad', as the software interprets my client's feelings. Really she should have the same, as that would be congruent or equal, as us psychotherapists say, but most counselling platforms leave that off – sessions can get very complicated otherwise. Of course, there is the option of a virtual meeting, in a virtual room, as an avatar – I shudder at the thought – or the ultimate, psychoconnect, where I connect my nervous system into my computing system which connects through Arianna's computing system directly into her nervous system, and I get to experience her thoughts and emotions first hand. I've not pursued getting licensed for that, thank goodness, as it is incredibly intense and can leave the psychotherapist in as bad a state as their client.

I remember during the First World Lockdown in 2020 when my internet service failed, the feeling of release that there was nothing I could do until it was fixed. I read and sketched and gardened, not that we have gardens like that anymore. Such technical failures are impossible now, in fact it's not possible to even get a light switch that isn't computer controlled – and I know because I tried!

I do so miss the old days in so many ways, none more so than when a client and I were in a room together. Quite apart from visual and auditory cues, one could sense feelings in a room, perhaps as vibrations emanating from each person. Sometimes I felt such sadness, the client's sadness, that it was like a cold water shower – not that we have those in the nifty fifties, the water shortages of global warming moved us all on to micro-particle and hot air cleansing systems. I used to be a dog trainer, and it was said that fear travelled down the lead. More than that, it ricocheted round the immediate area.

Subversive ideas nowadays, I don't speak of them, my license might get revoked. And of course, we don't have dogs any more, there is nowhere to walk them and they use too many resources. It was the Second World Lockdown of 2032 that saw the last of them off.

A plaintive, low pitched whine disturbs my train of thought, and a warm furry muzzle nudges my hand. That's Archie, wanting 'fed'. Archie is my robodog, and is very convincing, I can almost believe he is real. He is top of the range, with some of my last real dog's nervous tissue swaged into his circuitry so he behaves just like a dog, but he doesn't need to go to the toilet or exercise, and he doesn't get bored. I like to believe he likes to interact with me. He nuzzles me and wags his tail as I go to find his 'food'. Of course he doesn't need food, his gamma power source will power him long after I'm gone, but I have him programmed to ask for food, bark at drone deliveries and other dog-like behaviours. His synthetic skin and fur feel just like the real thing when I stroke or tickle him, and he rolls with delight, but of course he sheds no hair.

I miss real dogs – and real people. I am excited as my real life visit from my daughter is coming up soon. That happens every three years, and her drone pass has been issued. Oh, we meet up virtually all the time but it isn't the same. My grandchildren and their child won't come through, they don't see the point of meeting in person – they are scared of that closeness, my world is not their thing.

Bedtime soon. I feel I should use the cryo bed that the children got for me. Another 'advance' by another bright spark who realised that we sleep almost a third of our lives, so if we self-chill for that time, we can live a third of our life longer. So ninety is the new sixty, I think, ironically.

I am so reflective tonight, I was actually sixty when my client Arianna was born during the First World Lockdown – 1st WL. When I was the age she is now, thirty, my only computer was a Sinclair ZX Spectrum, and I had just got a state of the art mobile phone, the size and weight of a brick.

People met together without fear for coffee, walks, outings to cinemas and theatres. We climbed mountains and swam in the sea. If Arianna experienced any of those things, it was only briefly until the 2nd WL in 2032. That's when we realised for certain that life as my generation knew it would never be the same again.

I gently pat Archie's warm soft head and come to a decision. I'll not be using the cryo bed again. It's high time that Nature, what is left of it, takes its course.

**Author story note:** *I am a counsellor, and face to face work has stopped during lockdown, so I embarked on an online counselling course. It really is not 'my thing'!*

# Waking Up

**Abiy Orr**

---

It was always there, the Future,
A warm friendly thought in the back of the mind,
The magical journey to the land of intention,
The planned return to the places of love.
You would always be there.
It would always be possible.

Always there, the Future,
Just not accessible right now this minute:
Steadfast dreams of you and peace,
Of voyage and venture, country and seashore
As I get the children ready
And clatter through the washing up
And scribble down the shopping list
And hurtle out to work ...
Still mine for the taking, whenever the Future came.

Now I know differently.
No solid earth, no sturdy land,
No dealing in certainties here.
Beautiful still, but a gemstone bubble against the moon
The Future floats ahead of me,
Bright as the sunlight, fickle as the sea.

I yearn to grasp my certainties again,
Dread their disintegration at my touch.
O, pity this grieving fool
Who mistook a promising Future
For a promised one.

**Author story note:** *We're all autistic in my family, and my two sons are in residential care, the elder in supported accommodation, the younger at school. For years we've had a regular routine of visits to them and their holidays at home and we thought it would go on for ever. I wrote this in mid-April 2020 when Covid-19 had smashed that pattern and made it explosively clear to me that when we leave someone, we can never ever count on meeting them again in this world. I was complacent about what I valued. I'll never be that way again.*

# Signs
## Mark Edwards

Now Eck, ye kain aboot the changes?

Fit changes?

Nay mair Universal Joab Match.

Well, that makes sense. The universe is a big place. And as far as I kain yer best bet's still planet earth.

Eh?

Fit?

Ye said summin there.

Jist thinkin out loud man. Be cool.

Be cool! Are you on drugs?

Only the prescription kind.

Well, it's nay Universal Joab Match ony mair.

Well, that's a pity coz I've jist finished buildin a space rocket. Here, I taen a photo wi ma phone.

Bloody hell. Is that real?

Course it's real. In order ti fulfil ma work search commitment I intend tae visit distant galaxies. Hae a wee wurd wi the Martians and Venusians regardin potential employment opportunities.

Well, ye winna hae ti dae that noo, coz wiv changed it ti Find a Joab.

That disna suggest distant galaxies.

Ye're right. It disna.

A bittie a bugger efter me getherin in the materials. Then pittin it aa thegither.

I can only apologise.

The Ma's nay virrie happy coz it's takin up room in her shed.

Nivirmind that. Fit aboot Find a Joab?

Same thing. Different handle.

Exactly.

Fan they bringin in the firin squad?

Eh?

Might as well. Wir aa jist sittin aboot daen nuthin.

Wid ye like ti speak ti sumbdy?

I'm speakin tae you.

Aye but wiv got people ye can talk tae.

Fit people?

People that can help.

Aye but are they fit, as in female?

Fucksake. Jist sign here.

**Author story note:** *Canna mind.*

# Share your love of books...

Scottish Book Trust is an independent national charity. Our mission is to ensure people living in Scotland have equal access to books.

If you're enjoying this book, please consider making a donation so that everyone in Scotland has the opportunity to improve their life chances through books and the fundamental skills of reading and writing.

Visit **scottishbooktrust.com/support** to find out more.

# Hopes for a new decade

# New Beginnings
**Mary-Jean Parker**

On the first day I thought she would be unsure,
But she ran from room to room excited and giddy.
I painted the walls white, the colour of new beginnings
And hung tissue paper clouds above the bed.
She called it a pathway to a candy cane world.
Mermaids dangled from bed posts and unicorns lounged
   in corners.
We shared a picnic tea on the floor and chatted with her
   dolls.
We filled a pink flamingo air bed with cushions from the
   sofa,
wrapped ourselves in cosy blankets, and lay down to
   sleep.
I told her this is the house where dreams are made,
Where tales are told and wishes come true,
Where Santa leaves presents while children sleep
and fairies come to play at the bottom of the garden
I told her this is a house where bad things never happen.

I kissed her goodnight, crept from the room and sat
   down by her door.
I leant my head back, listened to the peace and exhaled,
Now, I could breathe
We are safe
We are together,
We are home.
We are free.

**Author story note**: *Domestic abuse has been called the
hidden pandemic in recent months, too many families
live in fear everyday of their lives.* New Beginnings *is a
story of survival, hope and better days ahead.*

# A Seashell Full of Grandkids
**Dini Armstrong**

---

The first question began to emerge when we dropped
off our youngest in her student accommodation, eager
to start her new life as an independent adult. Over the
years, we had waved off her older siblings, each time
with a chest full of pride and a throat full of tears that
we swallowed until we were out of sight. My husband
and I waved goodbye to our little ones, our ankle biters,
our tired little warm bellied babies, with the smell of
vanilla on their onesies when they woke from their
afternoon naps.

'Why are we living in this big empty house on
Anniesland Cross?'

It was a fair question, albeit shapeless at this point and
far from fully formed, a notion, unspoken yet clearly
perceptible. We had chosen the location due to its
proximity to good schools in the West End of Glasgow
– safe and close to their friends. But what would be the
attraction now? To us? To the kids? Once they'd started
travelling, once they'd fallen in love with partners and
scattered across the world – a new world, faster, brighter,
unrecognisable, a world that no longer belonged to us
but to them? What would be the justification for the cost
and effort of travelling all the way back here – to a busy
crossing in the north-west of Glasgow? Nothing wrong
with Anniesland, mind, it had been good to us, offering
its concrete pavements as a solid base for the kids to
hopscotch their way out of childhood. But why were we
paying a mortgage on a four-bedroom house, when there

were just the two of us left? So, within months, one of us, I don't remember who, asked the second question, driving along the shoreline of a small peninsula, about an hour from Glasgow:

'We would never move out this far, would we? I mean, we're city people, aren't we?'

It had started almost as a joke, a way to fill empty weekends: we searched online for houses near water, then took a day trip to look at them. Neither of us were entirely serious about this.

'I think it's the neighbour that's supposed to show us around. The guy isn't even home,' I said.

'I feel a bit bad about this,' my husband agreed. 'They're going to a lot of trouble, and it's not like we're actually going to buy it.'

'Do you want to cancel?'

'I don't know. Somehow that feels even meaner. I mean, they're already waiting for us.'

The closer we came, the more we felt like fraudsters. It was freezing cold, and only a few boats were moored on the loch, their silhouettes sharpened by the crisp winter light, colours faded to sepia.

'Worth it just to see all this,' we both agreed.

When we finally found the right house, I felt my heart pounding in my chest. We slowly rolled down the steep driveway, lined by trees on both sides. Gravel was crunching under our tyres, and an elderly lady appeared from one of the outhouses as soon as we got out of the car.

'Hello, lovely to meet you. I am Mhairie. Tom said you might be interested in buying his flat?'

It felt like lying when we nodded.

'Why don't I show you the outside of the house first?' she offered. We followed, sheepishly. She walked along the side of the house, explaining that it was split into three different flats, and that ours would be the one in the middle.

'The house was built in the 1870s, one of those Victorian children's homes, you know, for the Glasgow Fresh Air Fortnight.' We must have looked confused, because she explained: 'They offered two weeks of fun and fresh air to children from Glasgow's poorer areas.'

My husband took a deep and greedy breath. He smiled.

'No wonder they brought them here.'

I closed my eyes and tried to imagine the scene, twenty or so children, in white pinafores, playing, shrieking with fun.

When I opened them, I was struck by my husband's expression – the face of a child laying eyes on his first Christmas lights. I followed the direction of his open-mouthed gaze: The emerald green water of the loch, vast and achingly beautiful, lined by snow-topped hills above, with their counterparts reflected below the perfectly still surface. Only a few houses were dotted along the shore opposite. My husband and I looked at each other, and the next question formed, silently, telepathically:

'How the hell are we ever going to walk away from something this beautiful?'

'That's a nature reserve', Mhairie said. 'There's only one small village over there, with a lovely wee pub. My husband Charlie claims it takes him about half an hour to row across, and three hours to get back. One of life's mysteries, I guess.' We chuckled.

'Do you get any wildlife out here?' my husband asked.

'Of course! We get seals, porpoises, gannets, they even spotted a family of Orcas here once, but I didn't see them myself.'

I bent down and picked up a seashell, beautiful and spiral-shaped. How did this get here, I wondered? Did the waves wash up this high? Or did a seagull drop it onto the stones? I peeked inside and held my breath: I saw grandchildren playing on the lawn. I saw swings built by my husband, I saw him kick a ball around with a little girl, or boy. I saw kayaks lined up for fishing trips. I saw barbecues with freshly caught mackerel, and picnics on the grass. I saw our children and their partners sit on the bench, overlooking the loch, sipping a gin and tonic and letting the stress of adulthood wash away, more and more relaxed with each wave.

We were quiet on the drive back. Finally, my husband broke the silence with the last question:

'We're going to buy this, aren't we?' I felt for the seashell in my pocket, and the answer came easily:

'Yes. Yes, we are.'

**Author story note:** *This story is simply the truth. We did move in, and every day we are thankful that we found our way here. Whether our children decide to have kids or not, this place has become, and will hopefully continue to be, an oasis for all of us.*

# Visions of Loveliness
**Douglas Forrest**

---

The other day my son gave me a present. I could begin by asking you to guess what it was, but I suspect that unless you have a very weird imagination you are not likely to come up with the answer.

Here's a clue. It was so long it had to be coiled up and transported on a trailer.

Yes, it was a length of four-inch diameter perforated hose. It may not be what one would consider an exciting gift; original yes, but exciting? Perhaps not.

I suppose you are wondering why I was given this hose. The answer is quite simple. A frequently flooded garden.

Some people spend hours planning and then creating a garden pond. I didn't need to.

Throughout much of the winter and well through spring I have ponds galore and enough mud in which to hold a bog snorkelling competition.

A few years back I planted some willows because everyone knows that they love wet conditions. However, even the willows could not absorb all the water that accumulated in my garden.

When I was having one of my regular rants about my swamp, my son pointed out that he had a length of perforated hose that should help solve the problem.

As is frequently the case with solutions to problems, they arrive with inbuilt problems of their own. You see, for this hose to be effective it has to be buried. A suitable trench needs to be dug.

On the face of it that sounds simple. A few hours with a sharp spade and Bob's your uncle.

Well, he would be if it was simply a case of digging into nice topsoil. This was not something the builders of my house felt all that necessary at the time.

They must have had truck loads of rubble to dispose of and I'm sure you've guessed where they dumped it.

A few hours with a sharp spade has become days of hefting a seven-pound pick followed by even more days of a protesting back.

But one day, in the not too distant future, I hope the trench will be complete. Then I will require some gravel and the hose will be buried ready for next winter.

Next spring when I will be able to visit my local garden centre, I will be able to transform my former bog into terraced flower beds with colourful blooming borders.

Is this not a true vision of loveliness?

**Author story note:** *This story is based on what I am attempting to achieve now with my frequently flooded garden. It is hard to know how effective my work will be, but I live in hope!*

# Rainbow's End
**Alex Craig**

---

'You do know that there is no direct electricity supply to the cottage, just a generator? There is no mains water or sewerage. Water comes from the nearby stream and sometimes in the summer the stream can run low or dry up, so you need to be prepared if staying for any length of time.'

'Are you trying to put me off?' I asked.

'No, not at all,' the estate agent replied. 'But don't you want to view it?'

'I'm sure it will be perfect,' I reconfirmed. 'It's not going to be my main home, just a bit of a long-term rental bolthole that I can escape to.'

'It's called Rainbow's End.'

I chuckled to myself 'Rainbow's End', how appropriate! Things hadn't quite turned out the way that I thought they would. I had retired early from a public sector management job and quickly plunged into a downward spiral of staying up till the early hours, drinking too much, getting up at midday, of having no purpose. I had too much time to dwell on the possibilities of a post-operative cancer recurrence. Cancer had a lot to answer for!

Frayed and weary, I needed to find the will again, the will to do something great. If greatness was to elude me, mediocrity would be a starting point, at least I would be mediocre in the safety of the remote cottage with its creaking door and leaking roof.

'I'll take it,' I said to the estate agent.

With cancer follow-up test results clear, my self-rescue plan was rooted in being able to focus over the summer months on writing, something that I had always wanted to do but had never got around to. It might not have been a great plan, but it was something; it was a future which was better than no future at all.

Soon enough, the day came to collect the keys from the estate agent.

'Good luck up there, don't be getting snowed in,' said the estate agent as she handed me the brown envelope that contained one large key.

I drove for most of the day with the key in its brown envelope in pride of place on the passenger seat. I intended to stay for a month on this occasion, mainly to get the cottage organised, and to prepare for my longer summer stay. I arrived in Loch Carron, a pretty, Wester Ross village of white-washed cottages by the loch, continuing for a mile beyond the village and then down a gravel road by the loch side which snaked and wove its way to Rainbow's End.

My heart in my mouth as Rainbow's End came into view; grey stone and rock reflecting the glint of the loch. Stone and water, amidst heather dashed with pebble astride a long slither of silver sand. This wasn't a road to nowhere, it was a road to somewhere, I thought as I turned the key in the lock and opened the door to what would be a future yet to be charted.

I unloaded the car, brewed a large pot of good coffee and explored every nook and cranny. There was a kitchen of sorts with an old electric cooker, no washing machine, no fridge, no dishwasher. What had I been thinking, no dishwasher! The bathroom had seen better days, the living room small but cosy with a log burner and leaking roof and a tiny bedroom with a single bed that reeked of damp; the sofa would have to make do as my bed for the time being. Sleep!

The next morning, I was woken suddenly by loud whimpering; something was in the living room with me. I stumbled from the sofa, tripping over my own feet landing on the floor. A large unknown black dog was almost standing on top of me, wet and shaking and cold. I sprang to my feet, thinking that someone must be in the cottage.

'Hello,' I shouted at the top of my voice, to which the dog responded by barking as loud as it could.

'Sit!' I shouted at the dog, half expecting it to sink its teeth into my throat, but it didn't.

To my amazement the dog stopped barking and sat still as if waiting for further instruction. I checked the windows and the doors, I could hardly believe it, I had left the front door wide open the night before.

'Out!' I yelled at the dog, pointing towards the door. The dog seemed reluctant to move, but after I pointed to the door again, he slowly got up and limped towards the door, his hind leg bloodied by a snare of barbed wire that was still wrapped and embedded within it. 'Stop,' I said but the dog kept walking. 'Heel,' I said.

I loaded the dog into the car and took him to the vet, who confirmed that the dog had no chip and was severely malnourished and injured.

'Do you want me to put him to sleep? He's in quite a bad way,' the vet said.

I looked at the dog and the dog looked at me with his huge saucer eyes and I sighed. 'No, if you can patch him up, I will look after him until his owner can be found.' It was out of my mouth before I could stop myself. What was I doing?

A few months later I walked along the silver stretch

of sand by the loch, where I found a rock to perch upon and write. I watched the sun throw embers of pink, amber and ochre across the water as it slowly sunk below the silhouetted hills on the opposite bank. Bo sat at my feet; no one had claimed him in Loch Carron, no one knew where he had come from. As the day ended, Bo and I walked back together to our home at Rainbow's End. The future seemed wide open.

**Author story note:** *After having been diagnosed with kidney cancer I made a life-changing decision to give up my role as a senior manager within the public sector and concentrate on the things that I had always wanted to do. One of those things was to write. Initially, it was exceptionally difficult as I felt bereft of the career that I had built and the daily social interaction that the workplace brings. In addition having to deal with the ongoing anxiety with regard to the possibilities of the cancer returning. My decision to build a new future was the best decision that I could have ever made and the small adventure that I took in renting Rainbow's End and subsequently finding my good friend Bo helped bring that future to reality. I am doing just fine now.*

# A' Hò-rò Mu Dheire agus an t-Àm Ri Teachd

**Griogair MacThòmais**

---

Sgolt e e air muin an t-*cistern*, slighean geal far comhair
Mi fhèin 's mo charaid, nota truist' sinn deas am broinn
  an stàile
Loidhnichean fialaidh gan roinn eadar dithis
An club air bhoil am beus gar crith

Seo Dihaoine 's Disathairne fad bliadhna no dhà
Coma leinn an t-aithreachas a mhaireadh gu Dimàirt
Suas leis an duslach, sguab às an càrn
Ach an e seo e, an e seo dha-rìribh na tha an dàn?

Chan e – 's e seo, ma dh'fhaoidte, an trup mu dheire
Oir dh'eagraich mi mo phlana beatha
Cuiridh mi am baile mòr is a thaitneasan air chùl
Nì mise air a' Ghàidhealtachd, fàgaidh mi mo shaoghal

Dealaichear le caraidean a b' aithne bhon an sgoil
Seo a dh'fheumar dèanamh gus m' iomairt a chur gu dol
Tha gaol na tè gam tharraing suas a loch is garbh-chrìch
Ach cha bhean no leannan i mo ghràdh, 's i teanga tùs ar
  tìr.

Suas e is suas e le acras agus sannt
Tha gaoireag ruith tro fhèith is chois, tiugnamaid a
  dhanns
Tha oidhche a' dol na maidne ann am priobag bheag nan
  sùl
A dh'fhàs cho mòr ri gealaichean is sinn glacte anns an
  uaimh

Solas grèin a' dalladh is gar breaba' a bh' anns an dubhar
Tha barrachd ann na seo a-nis, 's i a' Ghàidhlig mo
  bheatha ùr
'Cumaidh sinn an touch, a laoich', a' fàgail slàn le Iain
  còir
Ach teansa gur e seo a' chrìoch air dàimhean a' bhaile
  mhòir

Na caoidh airson an fhògraich, na gabh truas air mo
  shon
Chan ionndrainn mi am baile mòr, cha robh mi ann ach
  seal
Am beàrn a bha nam shaoghal-sa nach d' fhuair sinn
  riamh san sgoil
Lìonar e le Gàidhlig ghrinn, ar n-eachdraidh is ar ceòl

Cuireamaid ar crìoch a-nis air an fhrith-rathad gheal
  mar sròin
Sguabar às gach creagag bhàn a chuireas sinn air bhoil
Is fàgaidh mi mo shoraidh slàn ceann là no 's dòcha dhà
Nì balach gallda air Innse Gall, an dèidh seo, mo
  shoraidh slàn.

# The Future and a Last Hurrah

He chopped it up upon the cistern, paths of gleaming
  white
Myself and a pal, notes rolled up inside the stall
Generous lines carved up
The club heaving and the muffled bass pounding

This has been my Friday and Saturday for a year or two
To hell with the hangover of regret that lasts till Tuesday
Up with the dust, guzzle up the heap
But is this really it, is this what's to be?

No – this is, quite probably, my last hurrah
I've been preparing an alternative life plan
I will put behind me the city and its charms
I'm making for the Highlands for a different kind of life

I will part from friends I've known from school
But that's what it will take to get my project off the
  ground
Her love is pulling me up to loch and hill and moor
But she is not a woman or a lover but my country's
  ancestral tongue

Up with it, up with it, with a greed and hunger
A tingling runs through veins and feet, I have to dance
Night becomes day in the blink of our eyes
That grew as big as planets while we were down in the
  cave

Sunlight blinding and thumping the creatures of the
  dark
There's more to life than this, my new life is a Gaelic one
'We'll keep in touch, bud', saying farewell to John
But this could be the end of friendships made in town

No laments for the exile, don't feel sorry for me
I won't miss the city, I was only there for a while
The void in my life that we never got at home, in school
Will be filled with Gaelic, our history and our song

Let's finish it together the white mountain track below
Hoover up every pale rock that sends us into artificial
  bliss
Then I'll say my goodbyes in a day, or maybe two
The lowland boy heads to the Hebrides, after this, my
  last hurrah.

# The Last Nicht Afore Lockdoon
**Harry**

---

Ah mind he wis a stunner. There wis me, saunterin up Sauchiehall Street on the last nicht afore lockdoon, oot ma face aefter geein laldy like a wis back in schuil.

'Where ye aff tae mate?' he says, cruisin up in a nice wee motor.

'Hame, just waitin oan the bus.' Am no tellin a lie tae say ah couldnae mind ma own name, let alane where a shud be staundin for a bus tae stoap.

'Here an ahl gie ye a lift up the road.'

'Nah, yer awrite, pal.' A looked awa, aff intae the chilly eastermaist distance. The black an orange lights ae Glesga flooterin as they do aefter a stint oan the bevy. A wisnae drookit, so why bather tae take ma chances endin up murthered in some manky dunny. Nae thanks. 'Shud be alang in a bit,' ah says.

'Naw it willnae, mate. There's a lockdoon. Nae buses.'

Whit in high heil wis this eejit oan aboot? Gallus tae hookie up tae perfect strangers, hingin oot his windae bletherin oan aboot lockdoons n that.

'Dinnae fash yersel, pal. Am only wantin tae gie yeh a lift hame.'

Ah looked this way n that. Up n doon. Nae bus. Not a scoobie. No even a dug. Hinkin a was prolly five meenits fae gettin lifted, ah let the bevy telt me whit tae dae.

'Maun then.'

Whit wud ma mither hink o this, then? Jumpin in motors wi haiverin bampots? Come tae hink ae it, Big Jan wouldnae hiv haud hauf the weans she haud wi out gettin her bahookie intae every bawheided bauchle's motor whit took a wrang turn intae the scheme. An' a was nuffin if no Big Jan's wean. Well, wan ae them at least.

'Whit's yer name?' he asks.

'Wha's you? The polis?'

'Ahm just tryin tae hauv a blether!'

'Aye? Trainin tae be a taxi driver? Well nae stars fae me, pal.'

'Yer hinkin ae Uber.'

'Aye well ah'll Uber you in a second, mate. Just drap us ower there. Ah'll walk.'

'From here tae Partick? Away ye go.' We drive oan tae a lay in the chat. 'Hame tae the missus, then?'

'Get tae,' ah says, geein him a sleekit grin. 'Ahm no a hunner.'

'Yeh dinnae hauv tae be auld tae be merrit.'

'An yersel? Dus yer missus ken yer oot geein lifts tae blootered lads? Or dae ye just dae that fur a laugh?'

Smicker he daed.

'Calm doon, ah wis only oot drappin aff a mate.'

Ah mate. Ah ken that wird. Twa in the morn, drivin aboot the empty toon. He'd no been drinkin, so whit aboot his mate? Bevyin alone, wis he? While auld mister blae een's sat an watched? Ah dinnae hink so. If it haud been a bird, he'd a said. Drappin aff ma bird, geein the missus a lift hame. But no, this wis the unkenable mate wi no name. Oh aye pal, ave got ye. Plain as parritch.

'How wis it the night?' He says, pauchlin a keek of me when another bloke wud be gairdin the road.

'Hoachin.'

'Aye, last nicht oot on the slash fur a guid wee bit.'

'Ye ken?'

'It's gain that way, aye. The warld shutten doon.

Grindin tae a hault. Awe ae us hame fur the Awmichtie kens how lang.'

'Aye well ahm no feart ae a stint in lockdoon.'

'Ah bet ye can dae six month staundin on yer heid.' But he dusnae say it tae be nestie. Naw, it was a wee bit aw understaundin eachither that wee bit mare.

'Sumfin like that.'

'Aye.'

Ave cut aboot the steamie. Ave staud in stowed oot crouds howfin out wabbit patter wi the lads. Wance it wis aboot lassies an hooch. Noo it's aw weans n hooses. Prolly hows ah can be hauf cut on a midweek nicht aefter a fest wan wi the boys.

Nae weans. Nae missus. The baith of us can dae six months nae bother. Nae bother at aw.

He pulls the motor in and a keek up at ma drawn windaes. Ah wid say come up, have a dram and a blether. But wit if it starts the nicht? Wit if we wake up an wee Nicola's oan the telly teltin us aw to dinnae move fur feart of fallin doon deid? Ah wonder if that wid be so bad.

Whit will ah say, seein him again? Or seein any ae us? Whit ye been uptae? No much, mate, yerself? Aye, too right no much. But ave been uptae sumfin. Ave been hinkin aboot that stunner. Braw an eesome. A weel-faured gausie wi hair as black as twa in the morn when first we met.

Cuz ahm hinkin ae us yont the noo. A wee hoose. Trips doon the watter. Twa dugs oan a corner sofa. Wan ae they big wans ye hauvetae hauve twa incomes fur. Cuz that's how twa blokes dae it. Life, ah mean. Yeh dinny find folk like that on yer phone, trawlin throu the dregs ae the scheme, feart tae swipe the wrang way oan a coupon ye ken an strike a riddy the next time yer staundin in the bookies or fae a bag a chips.

Aw this time ave been hinkin aboot faur yont flittin while starin at fower bare waws. Fallin doon that slidy brae ettlin ma future wi a puir bogle. Ah micht no huv a bawbee in ma pootch, but ave got sumfin else. Sumfin of ma ain whit nae corona an nae lockdoon can tak awa.

Ae fonde kiss.

An fine, we severed. Mibbe it'll be fareweel forever.

He said afore, 'Haud oan, lemme tak oot mah wallies.' Gave us baith a guid skelk. And the smuirich wis fonder fur it.

Even wi a bird, it's ne'er been couth fur men tae wither oan aboot recks o the hert. Twa gadgies taegither; well mibbe yer askin fur tribble. But ano wan hing weel. When a sees him again, ahm askin him oot.

**Author story note:** *This story was inspired by the last night out in Glasgow I had before the start of lockdown. I got a lift home from this guy driving by, and we kissed in his car before saying bye. That was the first and last time we saw each other as a few days later lockdown began. The story is about hoping for the future when this is over, and we might have a chance to see each other again. The story is written in Scots because, as a believer in the revival of the Scots language, I want to amplify the lives and stories of LGBTQ Scots in their native tongue.*

# Hopes for a New Decade
**Skye Wilson**

To kiss you at midnight – at ten midnights
of ten January firsts; at thousands of moments
in hundreds of mundane days; in dark,
and dappled sun, and burning brightness.

Well-packed suitcases, a second language,
weeks and months abroad with foreign booze,
tanned limbs tangled on crisp white hotel sheets.

To learn to hold a baby, or a job that affords me
expensive bras and last-minute plans: road trips,
days wasted playing cards, reading, making love,
and climbing Munroes in our ugliest clothes.

To decorate a Christmas tree together, to argue
and glitter through Decembers, chapped hands
held tight, and wax-sealed homemade cards.

A home. A little flat, with you, one day
a house: weeds blooming in the garden,
a wood fire, a piano, and a typewriter filled
with empty sheets ready to be poems.

**Author story note**: *I wrote it for my boyfriend at
Hogmanay. We're both in our final years of university,
so the future is looming in a way that's both exciting and
terrifying.*

# Share your love of books...

Scottish Book Trust is an independent national charity. Our mission is to ensure people living in Scotland have equal access to books.

If you've enjoyed this book, please consider making a donation so that everyone in Scotland has the opportunity to improve their life chances through books and the fundamental skills of reading and writing.

Visit **scottishbooktrust.com/support** to find out more.